Laravel Application Development Cookbook

Over 90 recipes to learn all the key aspects of Laravel, including installation, authentication, testing, and the deployment and integration of third parties in your application

Terry Matula

[PACKT] PUBLISHING

open source*
community experience distilled

BIRMINGHAM - MUMBAI

Laravel Application Development Cookbook

First published: October 2013

Production Reference: 1211013

Published by Packt Publishing Ltd.
Livery Place
35 Livery Street
Birmingham B3 2PB, UK.

ISBN 978-1-78216-282-7

www.packtpub.com

Cover Image by Sujay Gawand (sujaygawand@gmail.com)

Credits

Author
Terry Matula

Reviewers
Jason Lewis

Elan Marikit

Acquisition Editors
Mary Jasmine Nadar

Saleem Ahmed

Lead Technical Editor
Dayan Hyames

Technical Editors
Aparna Kumari

Sharvari Baet

Nadeem N. Bagban

Project Coordinator
Leena Purkait

Proofreaders
Stephen Copestake

Paul Hindle

Indexer
Tejal R. Soni

Production Coordinator
Nilesh R. Mohite

Cover Work
Nilesh R. Mohite

About the Author

Terry Matula is a web developer and Laravel advocate based in Austin, TX.

He's been a passionate computer enthusiast since he first played Oregon Trail on an Apple //e. He started programming in BASIC at a young age, making simple Scott Adams-like games on a Commodore Vic-20. Since then, he's worked as a developer using Flash/ActionScript, ASP.NET, PHP, and numerous PHP frameworks, with Laravel being his favorite by far.

He blogs web development tips and tricks at his website `http://terrymatula.com`

I'd like to thank Taylor Otwell for creating such a wonderful framework, and everyone in the Laravel community for being the most helpful and supportive group of people I've seen in the web development community. I'd also like to thank my beautiful wife Michelle for her continued encouragement and support, even when I was working 18 hour days to finish this book. Finally, I'd like to thank my son Evan, for keeping me grounded and being a shining light in my life.

About the Reviewers

Jason Lewis is a web developer and designer hailing from The Land Down Under (Australia). He's been using web technologies to develop websites for the past 7 years and is currently a huge Laravel evangelist. During the day, Jason is a professional firefighter, while at night he works hard on code and helps others learn to code. He's always willing to help and loves to write articles that guide others.

Elan Marikit is a software engineer with experience in many technologies, including PHP, JavaScript, MySQL, Linux, FreeBSD, and others. Elan has considerable experience in developing complex web-driven applications using an MVC-based framework such as CodeIgniter and Laravel. He is a Zend Certified Engineer for PHP 5.3 and is currently working in a Singapore-based startup company that builds scalable online travel portals with a focus in Southeast Asia.

www.PacktPub.com

Support files, eBooks, discount offers and more

You might want to visit www.PacktPub.com for support files and downloads related to your book.

Did you know that Packt offers eBook versions of every book published, with PDF and ePub files available? You can upgrade to the eBook version at www.PacktPub.com and as a print book customer, you are entitled to a discount on the eBook copy. Get in touch with us at service@packtpub.com for more details.

At www.PacktPub.com, you can also read a collection of free technical articles, sign up for a range of free newsletters and receive exclusive discounts and offers on Packt books and eBooks.

http://PacktLib.PacktPub.com

Do you need instant solutions to your IT questions? PacktLib is Packt's online digital book library. Here, you can access, read and search across Packt's entire library of books.

Why Subscribe?

- Fully searchable across every book published by Packt
- Copy and paste, print and bookmark content
- On demand and accessible via web browser

Free Access for Packt account holders

If you have an account with Packt at www.PacktPub.com, you can use this to access PacktLib today and view nine entirely free books. Simply use your login credentials for immediate access.

Table of Contents

Preface

Laravel has become one of the fastest growing PHP frameworks ever. With its expressive syntax and excellent documentation, it's easy to get a fully functioning web application up-and-running in very little time. Additionally, the use of modern PHP features makes Version 4 of Laravel very easy to customize to our own needs and also makes it easy for us to create a highly complex site if need be. It's a perfect blend of the simple and advanced.

This book covers merely a fraction of all that Laravel is capable of. Think of it more as a starting point, with code examples to get things working. Then customize them, add to them, or combine them to create your own applications. The possibilities are endless.

One of the best things about Laravel is the community. If you're ever stuck on a problem and doing a Google search isn't helping, there are always people willing to help out. You can find helpful community members on IRC (`#laravel` on Freenode) or the forums (`http://forums.laravel.io`) or you can contact the many Laravel users on Twitter.

Happy Laravel-ing!

What this book covers

Chapter 1, Setting Up and Installing Laravel, covers various ways to get Laravel up-and-running.

Chapter 2, Using Forms and Gathering Input, shows many ways to use forms in Laravel. It covers using Laravel's form class as well as some basic validation.

Chapter 3, Authenticating Your Application, demonstrates how to authenticate users. We'll see how to use OAuth, OpenId, and various social networks for authentication.

Chapter 4, Storing and Using Data, covers all things data, including how to use data sources other than a MySQL database.

Chapter 5, Using Controllers and Routes for URLs and APIs, introduces various routing methods in Laravel and how to make a basic API.

Chapter 6, Displaying Your Views, demonstrates how views work in Laravel. We'll also incorporate the Twig templating system and Twitter Bootstrap.

Chapter 7, Creating and Using Composer Packages, explains how to use packages in our app as well as how to create our own package.

Chapter 8, Using Ajax and jQuery, provides different examples of how to use jQuery in Laravel and how to make asynchronous requests.

Chapter 9, Using Security and Sessions Effectively, covers topics about securing our application and how to use sessions and cookies.

Chapter 10, Testing and Debugging Your App, shows how to include unit testing in our app with PHPUnit and Codeception.

Chapter 11, Deploying and Integrating Third-party Services into Your Application, introduces a number of third-party services and how we can include them in our application.

What you need for this book

This book basically requires a working LAMP stack (Linux, Apache, MySQL, and PHP). The web server is Apache 2, which can be found at `http://httpd.apache.org`. The recommended database server is MySQL 5.6, which can be downloaded from `http://dev.mysql.com/downloads/mysql`. The recommended minimum PHP version is 5.4, which is found at `http://php.net/downloads.php`.

For an all-in-one solution, there is also a WAMP server (`http://www.wampserver.com/en`) or XAMMP (`http://www.apachefriends.org/en/xampp.html`) for Windows or MAMP (`http://www.mamp.info/en/mamp-pro`) for Mac OS X.

Who this book is for

This book is designed for people with an intermediate knowledge of PHP. It would also be helpful to know the basics of another PHP framework or Version 3 of Laravel. Some knowledge of the MVC structure and object-oriented programming would also be beneficial.

Conventions

In this book, you will find a number of styles of text that distinguish between different kinds of information. Here are some examples of these styles, and an explanation of their meaning.

Code words in text, database table names, folder names, filenames, file extensions, pathnames, dummy URLs, user input, and Twitter handles, are shown as follows: "Then, we use the `artisan` command to generate a new key for us, and it's automatically saved in the correct file".

A block of code is set as follows:

```
Route::get('accounts', function()
{
  $accounts = Account::all();
  return View::make('accounts')->with('accounts',
    $accounts);
});
```

Any command-line input or output is written as follows:

```
php artisan key:generate
```

New terms and **important words** are shown in bold. Words that you see on the screen, in menus or dialog boxes for example, appear in the text like this: "After logging in to Pagodabox, click on the **New Application** tab".

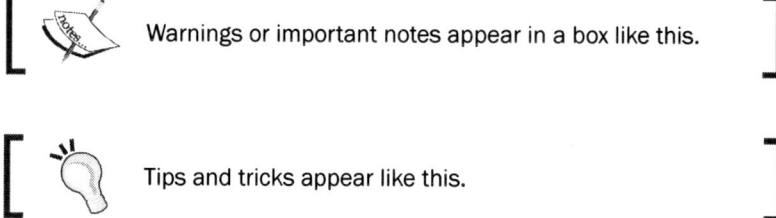

Warnings or important notes appear in a box like this.

Tips and tricks appear like this.

Reader feedback

Feedback from our readers is always welcome. Let us know what you think about this book—what you liked or may have disliked. Reader feedback is important for us to develop titles that you really get the most out of.

To send us general feedback, simply send an e-mail to feedback@packtpub.com, and mention the book title via the subject of your message.

If there is a topic that you have expertise in and you are interested in either writing or contributing to a book, see our author guide on www.packtpub.com/authors.

Customer support

Now that you are the proud owner of a Packt book, we have a number of things to help you to get the most from your purchase.

Downloading the example code

You can download the example code files for all Packt books you have purchased from your account at `http://www.packtpub.com`. If you purchased this book elsewhere, you can visit `http://www.packtpub.com/support` and register to have the files e-mailed directly to you.

Errata

Although we have taken every care to ensure the accuracy of our content, mistakes do happen. If you find a mistake in one of our books—maybe a mistake in the text or the code—we would be grateful if you would report this to us. By doing so, you can save other readers from frustration and help us improve subsequent versions of this book. If you find any errata, please report them by visiting `http://www.packtpub.com/submit-errata`, selecting your book, clicking on the **errata submission form** link, and entering the details of your errata. Once your errata are verified, your submission will be accepted and the errata will be uploaded on our website, or added to any list of existing errata, under the Errata section of that title. Any existing errata can be viewed by selecting your title from `http://www.packtpub.com/support`.

Piracy

Piracy of copyright material on the Internet is an ongoing problem across all media. At Packt, we take the protection of our copyright and licenses very seriously. If you come across any illegal copies of our works, in any form, on the Internet, please provide us with the location address or website name immediately so that we can pursue a remedy.

Please contact us at `copyright@packtpub.com` with a link to the suspected pirated material.

We appreciate your help in protecting our authors, and our ability to bring you valuable content.

Questions

You can contact us at `questions@packtpub.com` if you are having a problem with any aspect of the book, and we will do our best to address it.

1

Setting Up and Installing Laravel

In this chapter, we will cover:

- ▸ Installing Laravel as a git submodule
- ▸ Setting up a virtual host and development environment in Apache
- ▸ Creating "clean" URLs
- ▸ Configuring Laravel
- ▸ Using Laravel with Sublime Text 2
- ▸ Setting up your IDE to autocomplete Laravel's namespaces
- ▸ Using Autoloader to map a class name to its file
- ▸ Creating advanced Autoloaders with namespaces and directories

Introduction

In this chapter, we'll learn how to get Laravel up-and-running with ease and make sure it's simple to update when any core changes are made. We'll also get our development and coding environment set up to be very efficient so we can focus on writing great code and not have to worry about issues not related to our applications. Finally, we'll look at some ways to get Laravel to automatically do some work for us so we'll be able to extend our application in very little time.

Installing Laravel as a git submodule

There may be a time when we want to have our Laravel installation separate from the rest of our public files. In this case, installing Laravel as a git submodule would be a solution. This will allow us to update our Laravel files through git without touching our application code.

Getting ready

To get started, we should have our development server running as well as have git installed. In the server's web directory, create a `myapp` directory to hold our files. Installation will all be done in the command line.

How to do it...

To complete this recipe, follow these steps:

1. In your terminal or command line, navigate to the root of `myapp`. The first step is to initialize git and download our project files:

   ```
   $ git init
   $ git clone git@github.com:laravel/laravel.git
   ```

2. Since all we need is the `public` directory, move to `/laravel` and delete everything else:

   ```
   $ cd laravel
   $ rm -r app bootstrap vendor
   ```

3. Then, move back to the root directory, create a `framework` directory, and add Laravel as a submodule:

   ```
   $ cd ..
   $ mkdir framework
   $ cd framework
   $ git init
   $ git submodule add https://github.com/laravel/laravel.git
   ```

4. Now we need to run Composer to install the framework:

   ```
   php composer.phar install
   ```

 More information about installing Composer can be found at `http://getcomposer.org/doc/00-intro.md`. The rest of the book will assume we're using `composer.phar`, but we could also add it globally and simply call it by typing `composer`.

5. Now, open `/laravel/public/index.php` and find the following lines:

```
require __DIR__.'/../bootstrap/autoload.php';

$app = require_once __DIR__.'/../bootstrap/start.php';
```

6. Change the preceding lines to:

```
require __DIR__.'/../../framework/laravel/bootstrap/
    autoload.php';

$app = require_once __DIR__.'/../../framework/laravel/
    bootstrap/start.php';
```

How it works...

For many, simply running `git clone` would be enough to get their project going. However, since we want to have our framework act as a submodule, we need to separate those files from our project.

First, we download the files from GitHub, and since we don't need any of the framework files, we can delete everything but our public folder. Then, we create our submodule in the `framework` directory and download everything there. When that's complete, we run `composer install` to get all our vendor packages installed.

To get the framework connected to our application, we modify `/laravel/public/index.php` and change the `require` paths to our framework directory. That will let our application know exactly where the framework files are located.

There's more...

One alternative solution is to move the `public` directory to our server's root. Then, while updating our `index.php` file, we'll use `__DIR__ . '/../framework/laravel/bootstrap'` to include everything correctly.

Setting up a virtual host and development environment in Apache

When developing our Laravel app, we'll need a web server to run everything. In PHP 5.4 and up, we can use the built-in web server, but if we need some more functionality, we'll need a full web stack. In this recipe, we'll be using an Apache server on Windows, but any OS with Apache will be similar.

Getting ready

This recipe requires a recent version of WAMP server, available at `http://wampserver.com`, though the basic principle applies to any Apache configuration on Windows.

How to do it...

To complete this recipe, follow these steps:

1. Open the WAMP Apache `httpd.conf` file. It is often located in `C:/wamp/bin/apache/Apach2.#.#/conf`.

2. Locate the line `#Include conf/extra/httpd-vhosts.conf` and remove the first #.

3. Move to the `extra` directory, open the `httpd-vhosts.conf` file, and add the following code:

```
<VirtualHost *:80>
    ServerAdmin {your@email.com}
    DocumentRoot "C:/path/to/myapp/public"
    ServerName myapp.dev
    <Directory "C:/path/to/myapp/public">
        Options Indexes FollowSymLinks
        AllowOverride all
        # onlineoffline tag - don't remove
        Order Deny,Allow
        Deny from all
        Allow from 127.0.0.1
    </Directory>
</VirtualHost>
```

4. Restart the Apache service.

5. Open the Windows hosts file, often in `C:/Windows/System32/drivers/etc`, and open the file `hosts` in a text editor.

6. At the bottom of the file, add the line `127.0.0.1   myapp.dev`.

How it works...

First, in the Apache config file `httpd.conf`, we uncomment the line to allow the file to include the `vhosts` configuration files. You can include the code directly in the `httpd.conf` file, but this method keeps things more organized.

In the `httpd-vhosts.conf` file, we add our VirtualHost code. `DocumentRoot` tells the server where the files are located and `ServerName` is the base URL that the server will look for. Since we only want to use this for our local development, we make sure to only allow access to the localhost with the IP `127.0.0.1`.

In the `hosts` file, we need to tell Windows which IP to use for the `myapp.dev` URL. After restarting Apache and our browser, we should be able to go to `http://myapp.dev` and view our application.

There's more...

While this recipe is specific to Windows and WAMP, the same idea can be applied to most Apache installations. The only difference will be the location of the `httpd.conf` file (in Linux Ubuntu, it's in `/etc/apache2`) and the path to the `public` directory for DocumentRoot (in Ubuntu, it might be something like `/var/www/myapp/public`). The `hosts` file for Linux and Mac OS X will be located in `/etc/hosts`.

Creating "clean" URLs

When installing Laravel, the default URL we will use is `http://{your-server}/public`. If we decide to remove `/public`, we can use Apache's `mod_rewrite` to change the URL.

Getting ready

For this recipe, we just need a fresh installation of Laravel and everything running on a properly configured Apache server.

How to do it...

To complete this recipe, follow these steps:

1. In our app's root directory, add a `.htaccess` file and use this code:

```
<IfModule mod_rewrite.c>
    RewriteEngine On
    RewriteRule ^(.*)$ public/$1 [L]
</IfModule>
```

2. Go to `http://{your-server}` and view your application.

How it works...

This simple bit of code will take anything we add in the URL and direct it to the `public` directory. That way, we don't need to manually type in `/public`.

There's more...

If we decide to move this application to a production environment, this is not the best way to accomplish the task. In that case, we would just move our files outside the web root and make /public our root directory.

Configuring Laravel

After installing Laravel, it's pretty much ready to go without much need for configuration. However, there are a few settings we want to make sure to update.

Getting ready

For this recipe, we need a regular installation of Laravel.

How to do it...

To complete this recipe, follow these steps:

1. Open /app/config/app.php and update these lines:

```
'url' => 'http://localhost/',
'locale' => 'en',
'key' => 'Seriously-ChooseANewKey',
```

2. Open app/config/database.php and choose your preferred database:

```
'default' => 'mysql',
'connections' => array(
    'mysql' => array(
        'driver'    => 'mysql',
        'host'      => 'localhost',
        'database'  => 'database',
        'username'  => 'root',
        'password'  => '',
        'charset'   => 'utf8',
        'collation' => 'utf8_unicode_ci',
        'prefix'    => '',
        ),
    ),
```

3. In the command line, go to the root of the app and make sure the storage folder is writable:

```
chmod -R 777 app/storage
```

How it works...

Most of the configuration will happen in the `/app/config/app.php` file. While setting the URL isn't required, and Laravel does a great job figuring it out without setting it, it's always good to remove any work from the framework that we can. Next, we set our location. If we choose to provide **localization** in our app, this setting will be our default. Then, we set our application key, since it's best to not keep the default.

Next, we set which database driver we'll be using. Laravel comes with four drivers out of the box: mysql, sqlite, sqlsrv (MS SQL Server), and pgsql (Postgres).

Finally, our `app/storage` directory will be used for keeping any temporary data, such as sessions or cache, if we choose. To allow this, we need to make sure the app can write to the directory.

There's more...

For an easy way to create a secure application key, remove the default key and leave it empty. Then, in your command line, navigate to your application root directory and type:

```
php artisan key:generate
```

That will create a unique and secure key and automatically save it in your configuration file.

Using Laravel with Sublime Text 2

One of the most popular text editors used for coding is Sublime Text. Sublime has many features that make coding fun, and with plugins, we can add in Laravel-specific features to help with our app.

Getting ready

Sublime Text 2 is a popular code editor that is very extensible and makes writing code effortless. An evaluation version can be downloaded from `http://www.sublimetext.com/2`.

We also need to have the Package Control package installed and enabled in Sublime, and that can be found at `http://wbond.net/sublime_packages/package_control/installation`.

How to do it...

For this recipe, follow these steps:

1. In your menu bar, go to **Preferences** then **Package Control**:

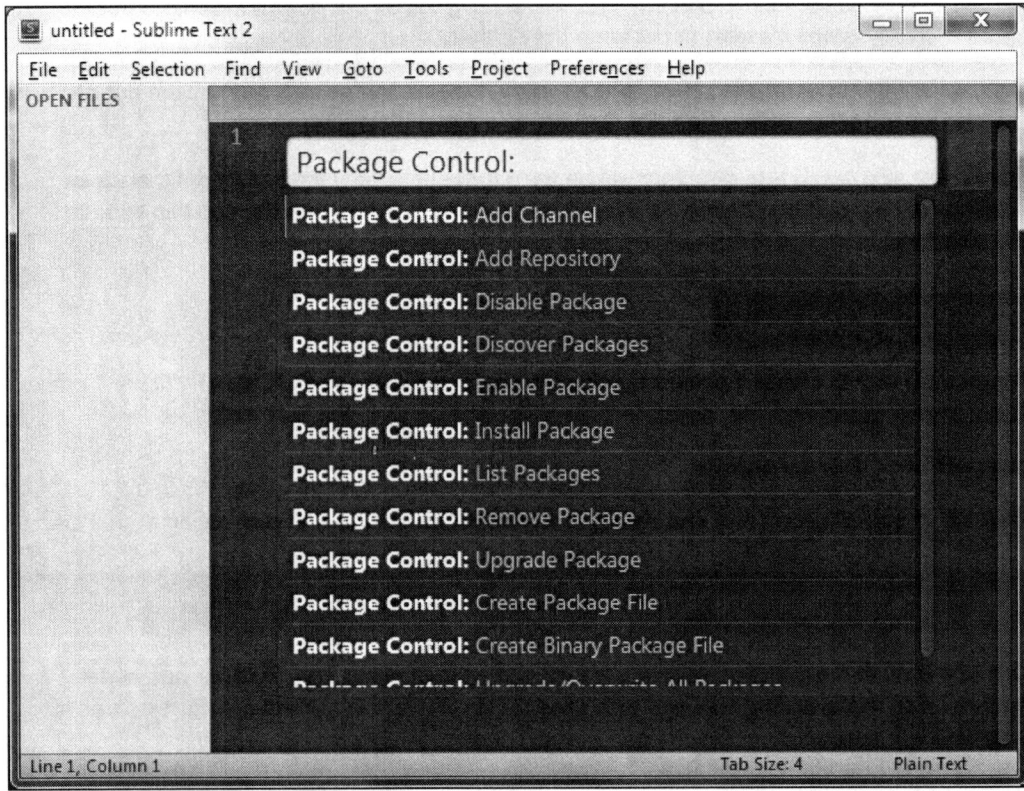

2. Choose **Install Package**:

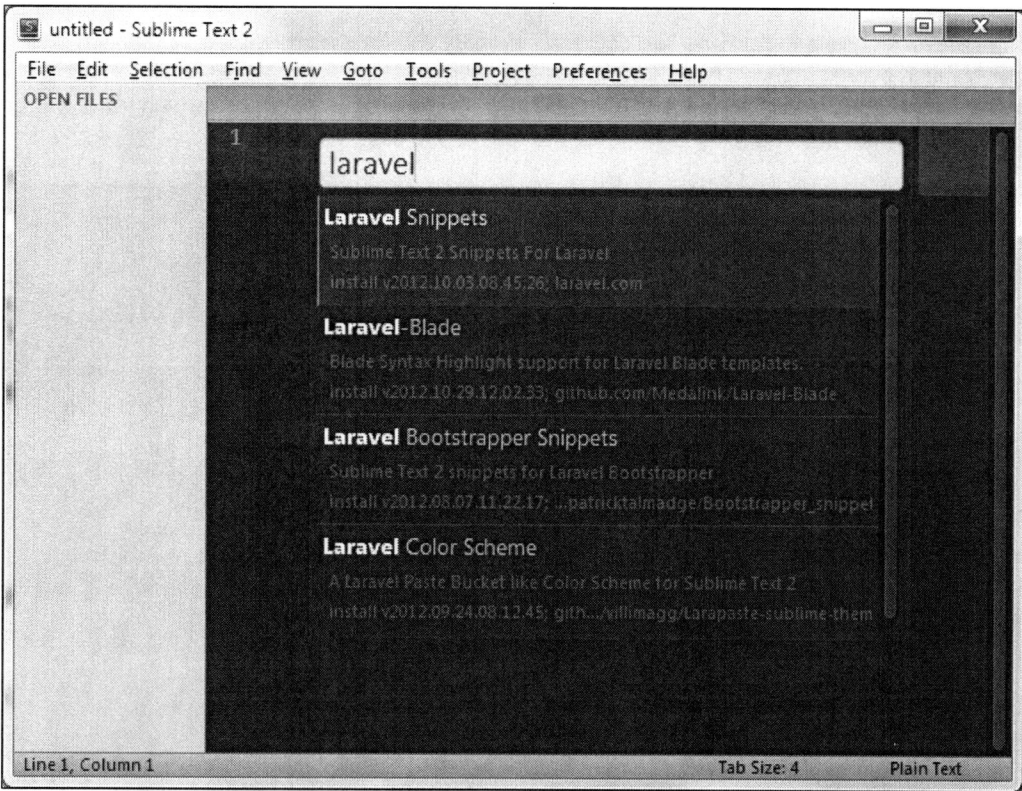

3. Search for `laravel` to see the listing. Choose **Laravel 4 Snippets** and let it install. After it's complete, choose **Laravel-Blade** and install it.

How it works...

The Laravel snippets in Sublime Text 2 greatly simplify writing common code, and it includes pretty much everything we'll need for application development. For example, when creating a route, simply start typing `Route` and a list will pop up allowing us to choose which route we want, which then automatically completes the rest of the code we need.

```
34   Route::get('/', function()
35   {
36       return View::make('home.index');
37   });
38
39   Route
40           Route          Laravel: Route::any()
41           Route    Laravel: Route::controller()
42   /*      Route        Laravel: Route::delete()
43   |----   Route        Laravel: Route::filter()
44   | App   Route        Laravel: Route::get()
45   |----   Route        Laravel: Route::group()     Laravel uses an
46   |       Route        Laravel: Route::post()      e to modify this
47   | To    Route        Laravel: Route::put()       tion.
48   | sys
49   | you
50   |
51   | Similarly, we use an event to handle the display of 500 I
52   | within the application. These errors are fired when there
```

There's more...

Installing the Laravel-Blade package is helpful if we use the Blade template system that comes with Laravel. It recognizes Blade code in the files and will automatically highlight the syntax.

Setting up your IDE to autocomplete Laravel's namespaces

Most **IDEs** (**Integrated Development Environment**) have some form of code completion as part of the program. To get Laravel's namespaces to autocomplete, we may need to help it recognize what the namespaces are.

Getting ready

For this recipe, we'll be adding namespaces to the NetBeans IDE, but the process will be similar with others.

How to do it...

Follow these steps to complete this recipe:

1. Download the following pre-made file that lists the Laravel namespaces: https://gist.github.com/barryvdh/5227822.

2. Create a folder anywhere on your computer to hold this file. For our purposes, we'll add the file to C:/ide_helper/ide_helper.php:

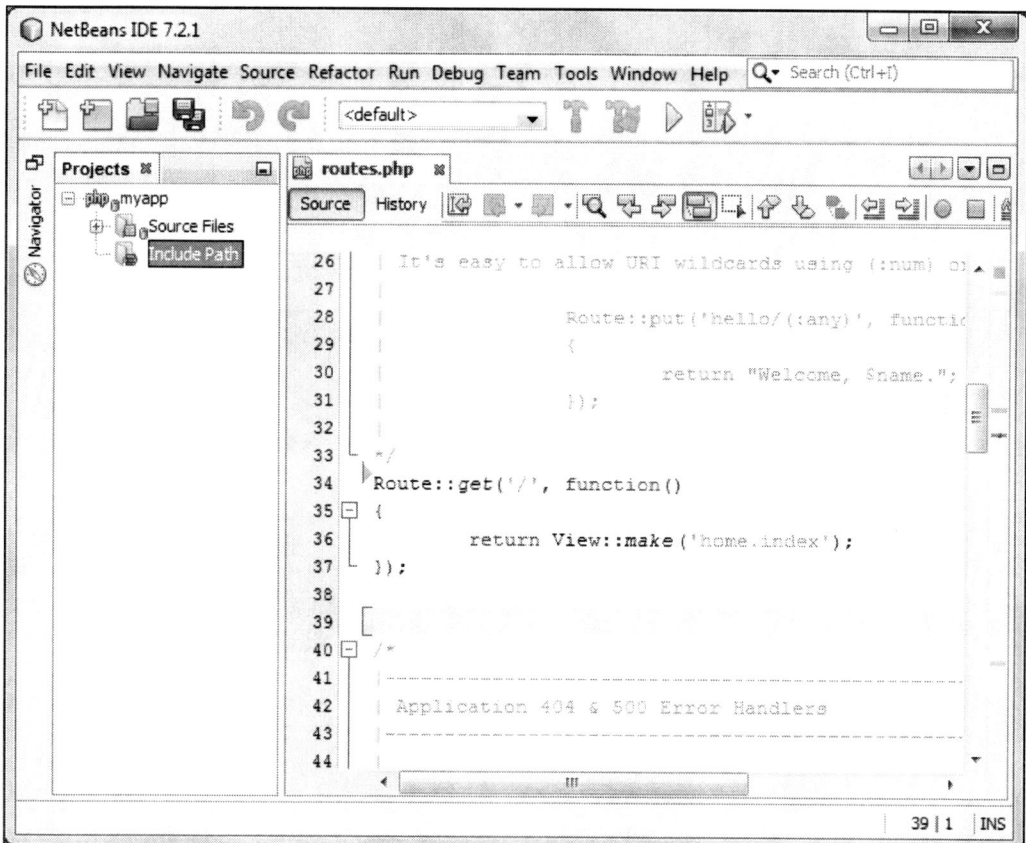

3. After creating a project with the Laravel framework, navigate to **File | Project Properties | PHP Include Path**:

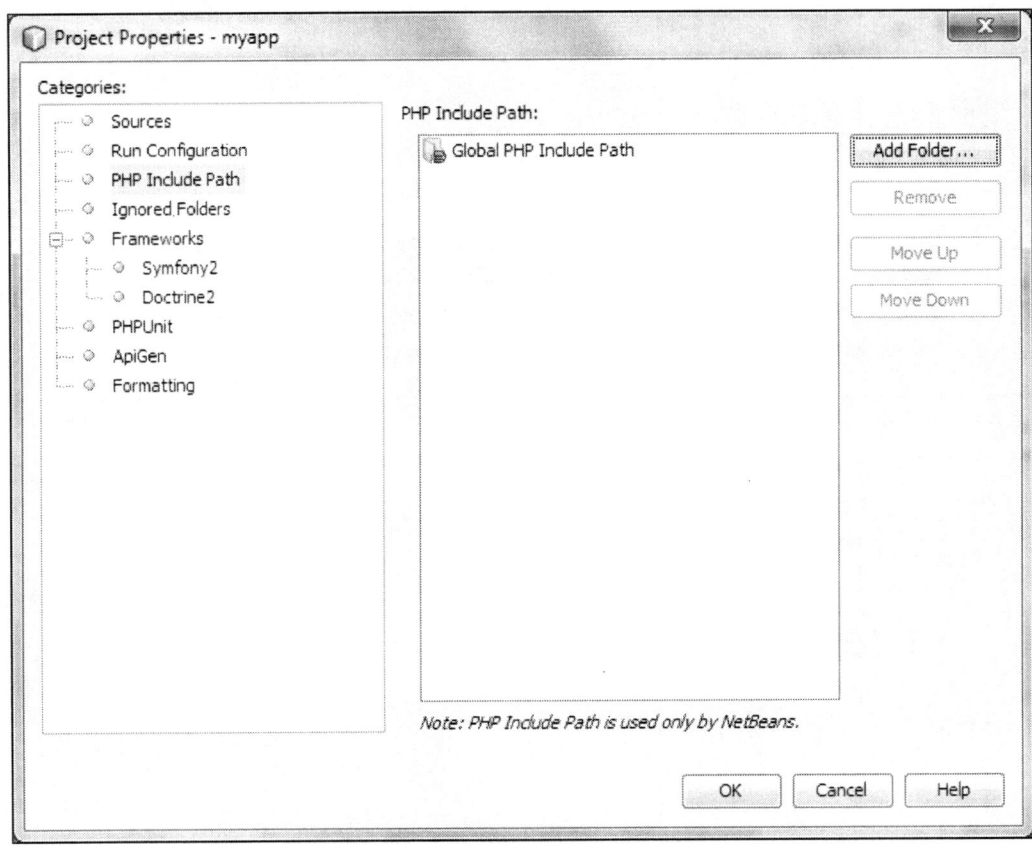

4. Click on **Add Folder...** and then add the folder at C:/ide_helper.

5. Now when we start typing the code, the IDE will automatically suggest code to complete:

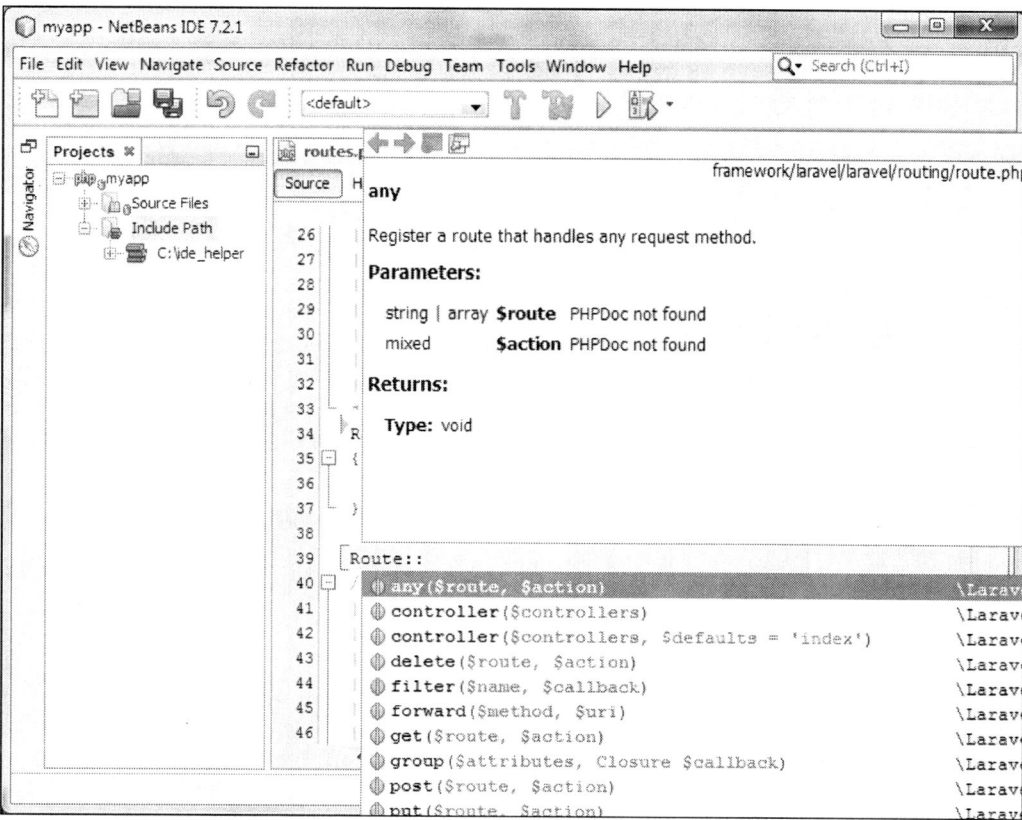

How it works...

Some IDEs need help understanding the syntax of a framework. To get NetBeans to understand, we download a list of all the Laravel classes and options. Then, when we add it to the Include Path, NetBeans will automatically check the file and show us the autocomplete options.

There's more...

We can have the documents downloaded and updated automatically using Composer. For installation instructions, visit https://github.com/barryvdh/laravel-ide-helper.

Using Autoloader to map a class name to its file

Using Laravel's ClassLoader, we can easily include any of our custom class libraries in our code and have them readily available.

Getting ready

For this recipe, we need to set up a standard Laravel installation.

How to do it...

To complete this recipe, follow these steps:

1. In the Laravel /app directory, create a new directory named custom, which will hold our custom classes.

2. In the custom directory, create a file named MyShapes.php and add this simple code:

```php
<?php
class MyShapes {
    public function octagon()
    {
        return 'I am an octagon';
    }
}
```

3. In the /app/start directory, open global.php and update ClassLoader so it looks like this:

```php
ClassLoader::addDirectories(array(

    app_path().'/commands',
    app_path().'/controllers',
    app_path().'/models',
    app_path().'/database/seeds',
    app_path().'/custom',

));
```

4. Now we can use that class in any part of our application. For example, if we create a route:

```php
Route::get('shape', function()
{
    $shape = new MyShapes;
    return $shape->octagon();
});
```

How it works...

Most of the time, we will use Composer to add packages and libraries to our app. However, there may be libraries that aren't available through Composer or custom libraries that we want to keep separate. To accomplish this, we need to dedicate a spot to hold our class libraries; in this case, we create a directory named `custom` and put it in our `app` directory.

Then we add our class files, making sure the class names and filenames are the same. This could either be classes we create ourselves or maybe even a legacy class that we need to use.

Finally, we add the directory to Laravel's ClassLoader. When that's complete, we'll be able to use those classes anywhere in our application.

See also

▶ The *Creating advanced Autoloaders with namespaces and directories* recipe

Creating advanced Autoloaders with namespaces and directories

If we want to be sure that our custom classes don't conflict with any other class in our app, we will need to add them to a namespace. Using the PSR-0 standard and Composer, we can easily autoload these classes into Laravel.

Getting ready

For this recipe, we need to set up a standard Laravel installation.

How to do it...

To complete this recipe, follow these steps:

1. Inside the `/app` directory, create a new directory named `custom`, and inside of `custom`, create a directory named `Custom`, and in `Custom`, create a directory named `Shapes`.

2. Inside the `/app/custom/Custom/Shapes` directory, create a file named `MyShapes.php` and add this code:

```php
<?php namespace Custom\Shapes;

class MyShapes {
    public function triangle()
    {
        return 'I am a triangle';
    }
}
```

3. In the root of the application, open the `composer.json` file and locate the `autoload` section. Update it so it looks like this:

```
"autoload": {
    "classmap": [
    "app/commands",
        "app/controllers",
        "app/models",
        "app/database/migrations",
        "app/database/seeds",
        "app/tests/TestCase.php",
    ],
    "psr-0": {
        "Custom": "app/custom"
    }
}
```

4. Open the command line and run `dump-autoload` on Composer:

```
php composer.phar dump-autoload
```

5. Now we can call that class by using its namespace. For example, if we create a route:

```
Route::get('shape', function()
{
    $shape = new Custom\Shapes\MyShapes;
    return $shape->triangle();
});
```

How it works...

Namespaces are a powerful addition to PHP, and they allow our classes to be used without us having to worry about their class names interfering with other class names. By autoloading namespaces in Laravel, we could create a complex group of classes and never have to worry about class names conflicting with other namespaces.

For our purposes, we're loading the custom class through composer, and the PSR-0 standard of autoloading.

There's more...

To further extend the use of our namespaced class, we could use the **IoC** to bind it to our app. More information can be found in the Laravel documentation at `http://laravel.com/docs/ioc`.

See also

▶ The *Using Autoloader to map a class name to its file* recipe

2
Using Forms and Gathering Input

In this chapter, we will cover:

- ▶ Creating a simple form
- ▶ Gathering form input to display on another page
- ▶ Validating user input
- ▶ Creating a file uploader
- ▶ Validating a file upload
- ▶ Creating a custom error message
- ▶ Adding a "honey pot" to a form
- ▶ Uploading an image using Redactor
- ▶ Cropping an image with Jcrop
- ▶ Creating an autocomplete text input
- ▶ Making a CAPTCHA style spam catcher

Introduction

In this chapter, we'll learn about using forms in Laravel, and how to accomplish some typical tasks. We'll begin with some simple form validation and file uploads, and move on to incorporating some frontend tools, such as Redactor and jCrop, into Laravel.

Creating a simple form

One of the most basic aspects of any web application is the form. Laravel provides easy ways to build HTML for our forms.

Getting ready

To get started, we need a fresh installation of Laravel.

How to do it...

To complete this recipe, follow these steps:

1. In the `app/views` folder, create a new `userform.php` file.

2. In `routes.php`, create a route to load the view:

    ```
    Route::get(userform, function()
    {
        return View::make('userform');
    });
    ```

3. In the `userform.php` view, create a form using the following code:

    ```
    <h1>User Info</h1>
    <?= Form::open() ?>
    <?= Form::label('username', 'Username') ?>
    <?= Form::text('username') ?>
    <br>
    <?= Form::label('password', 'Password') ?>
    <?= Form::password('password') ?>
    <br>
    <?= Form::label('color', 'Favorite Color') ?>
    <?= Form::select('color', array('red' => 'red', 'green' =>
        'green', 'blue' => 'blue')) ?>
    <br>
    <?= Form::submit('Send it!') ?>
    <?= Form::close() ?>
    ```

View your form in the web page, by going to `http://{your-server}/userform` (where `{your-server}` is the name of your server).

How it works...

For this task, we created a simple form using Laravel's built-in `Form` class. This allows us to easily create form elements with minimal code, and it's W3C (World Wide Web Consortium) compliant.

First, we open the form. Laravel automatically creates the `<form>` html, including the action, the method, and the accept-charset parameters. When there are no options passed in, the default action is the current URL, the default method is `POST`, and the charset is taken from the application config file.

Next we create normal text and password input fields, along with their labels. The first parameter in the label is the name of the text field and the second is the actual text to print. In the form builder, the label should appear before the actual form input.

The form select requires a second parameter, an array of the value in the drop-down box. In this example, we're creating an array using the `'key' => 'value'` syntax. If we want to create option groups, we just need to create nested arrays.

Finally, we create our Submit button and close the form.

There's more...

Most of Laravel's form methods can also include parameters for a default value and custom attributes (classes, IDs, and so on). We could also use `Form::input()` for many fields, if we didn't want to use the specific methods. For example, we could have `Form::input('submit', NULL, 'Send it!')` to create a submit button.

See also

- ▶ The *Gathering form input to display on another page* recipe

Gathering form input to display on another page

After a user submits a form, we need to be able to take that information and pass it to another page. This recipe shows how we can use Laravel's built-in methods to handle our POST data.

Getting ready

We'll need the simple form set up from the *Creating a simple form* section.

How to do it...

Follow these steps to complete this recipe:

1. Create a route to handle the POST data from the form:

```
Route::post('userform', function()
{
    // Process the data here
    return Redirect::to('userresults')-
        >withInput(Input::only('username', 'color'));
});
```

2. Create a route to redirect to, and to display the data:

```
Route::get('userresults', function()
{
    return 'Your username is: ' . Input::old('username')
        . '<br>Your favorite color is: '
        . Input::old('color');
});
```

How it works...

In our simple form, we're POSTing the data back to the same URL, so we need to create a route that accepts POST using the same path. This is where we would do any processing of the data, including saving to a database or validating the input.

In this case, we simply want to pass the data to the next page. There are a number of ways to accomplish this. For example, we could use the Input class's flashOnly() method:

```
Route::post('userform', function()
{
    Input::flashOnly('username', 'color');
    return Redirect::to('userresults');
});
```

However, we're using a shortcut that Laravel provides, and only passing along two of the three form fields we asked for.

On the next page, we use Input::old() to display the flashed input.

See also

▶ The *Creating a simple form* recipe

Validating user input

In most web applications, there will be certain form fields that are required to process the form. We also want to be sure that all the e-mail addresses are formatted correctly, or the input must have a certain number of characters. Using Laravel's `Validator` class, we can check for these rules and let the user know if something is not correct.

Getting ready

For this recipe, we just need a standard installation of Laravel.

How to do it...

To complete this recipe, follow these steps:

1. Create a route to hold the form:

```
Route::get('userform', function()
{
    return View::make('userform');
});
```

2. Create a view named `userform.php` and add a form:

```
<h1>User Info</h1>
<?php $messages = $errors->all('<p
    style="color:red">:message</p>') ?>
<?php
foreach ($messages as $msg)
{
    echo $msg;
}
?>
<?= Form::open() ?>
<?= Form::label('email', 'Email') ?>
<?= Form::text('email', Input::old('email')) ?>
<br>
<?= Form::label('username', 'Username') ?>
<?= Form::text('username', Input::old('username')) ?>
<br>
<?= Form::label('password', 'Password') ?>
<?= Form::password('password') ?>
<br>
<?= Form::label('password_confirm', 'Retype your Password')
    ?>
```

```
<?= Form::password('password_confirm') ?>
<br>
<?= Form::label('color', 'Favorite Color') ?>
<?= Form::select('color', array('red' => 'red', 'green' =>
    'green', 'blue' => 'blue'), Input::old('color')) ?>
<br>
<?= Form::submit('Send it!') ?>
<?php echo Form::close() ?>
```

3. Create a route that handles our POST data and validates it:

```
Route::post('userform', function()
{
    $rules = array(
        'email' => 'required|email|different:username',
        'username' => 'required|min:6',
        'password' => 'required|same:password_confirm'
    );
    $validation = Validator::make(Input::all(), $rules);

    if ($validation->fails())
    {
        return Redirect::to('userform')-
            >withErrors($validation)->withInput();
    }

    return Redirect::to('userresults')->withInput();

});
```

4. Create a route to handle a successful form submission:

```
Route::get('userresults', function()
{
    return dd(Input::old());
});
```

How it works...

In our form page, we begin by checking if there are any errors and displaying them if found. Inside the error, we can set the default style for each error message. We also have the option of checking for and displaying errors for individual fields using $errors->get('email'). The $errors variable is automatically created by Laravel if it detects a flashed error.

Next, we create our form. In the last parameter of the form elements, we're getting Input::old(), which we use to store the previous input if the validation happens to fail. That way, the user won't need to keep filling out the entire form.

We then create a route where the form is POSTed, and set up our validation rules. In this case, we use the required rule for `email`, `username`, and `password`, to make sure something is typed into those fields.

The `email` field also gets the `email` rule, which uses PHP's built-in `FILTER_VALIDATE_EMAIL` filter of the `filter_var` function. The `email` field must also not be the same as the `username` field. The `username` field uses the size validation to check for at least six characters. Then the `password` field checks the value of the `password_confirm` field and makes sure they're the same.

Then, we create the validator and pass in all of the form data. If any of those rules aren't met, we navigate the user back to the form, and also send back any validation error messages as well as the original form input.

If the validation passes, we go to the next page using Laravel's `dd()` helper function, which uses `var_dump()` to show the form values on the page.

See also

▶   *The Creating a simple form recipe*

Creating a file uploader

There may be times when we'd like the user to upload a file to our server. This recipe shows how Laravel can handle file uploads through a web form.

Getting ready

To create a file uploader, we need a standard version of Laravel installed.

How to do it...

To complete this recipe, follow these steps:

1. Create a route in our `routes.php` file to hold the form:

    ```
    Route::get('fileform', function()
    {
        return View::make('fileform');
    });
    ```

2. Create the `fileform.php` View in our `app/views` directory:

    ```
    <h1>File Upload</h1>
    <?= Form::open(array('files' => TRUE)) ?>
    <?= Form::label('myfile', 'My File') ?>
    ```

```
<br>
<?= Form::file('myfile') ?>
<br>
<?= Form::submit('Send it!') ?>
<?= Form::close() ?>
```

3. Create a route to upload and save the file:

```
Route::post('fileform', function()
{
    $file = Input::file('myfile');
    $ext = $file->guessExtension();
    if ($file->move('files', 'newfilename.' . $ext))
    {
        return 'Success';
    }
    else
    {
        return 'Error';
    }
});
```

How it works...

In our View, we use `Form::open ()` and pass in an array with `'files' => TRUE` that automatically sets the enctype in the `Form` tag; then we add a form field to take the file. Without using any other parameters in `Form::open ()`, the form will use the default method of POST and action of the current URL. `Form::file ()` is our input field to accept the files.

Since our form is posting to the same URL, we need to create a route to accept the POST input. The `$file` variable will hold all the file information.

Next, we want to save the file with a different name but first we need to get the extension of the uploaded file. So we use the `guessExtension ()` method, and store that in a variable. Most of the methods for using files are found in Symfony's File libraries.

Finally, we move the file to its permanent location using the file's `move ()` method, with the first parameter being the directory where we will save the file; the second is the new name of the file.

If everything uploads correctly, we show `'Success'`, and if not we show `'Error'`.

See also

► The *Validating a file upload* recipe

Validating a file upload

If we want to allow users to upload a file through our web form, we may want to restrict which kind of file they upload. Using Laravel's `Validator` class, we can check for a specific file type, and even limit the upload to a certain file size.

Getting ready

For this recipe, we need a standard Laravel installation, and an example file to test our upload.

How to do it...

Follow these steps to complete this recipe:

1. Create a route for the form in our `routes.php` file:

```
Route::get('fileform', function()
{
    return View::make('fileform');
});
```

2. Create the form view:

```
<h1>File Upload</h1>
<?php $messages =  $errors->all('<p style="color:red">:message</
p>') ?>
<?php
foreach ($messages as $msg)
{
    echo $msg;
}
?>
<?= Form::open(array('files' => TRUE)) ?>
<?= Form::label('myfile', 'My File (Word or Text doc)') ?>
<br>
<?= Form::file('myfile') ?>
<br>
<?= Form::submit('Send it!') ?>
<?= Form::close() ?>
```

3. Create a route to validate and process our file:

```
Route::post('fileform', function()
{
    $rules = array(
        'myfile' => 'mimes:doc,docx,pdf,txt|max:1000'
    );
```

```
        $validation = Validator::make(Input::all(), $rules);

        if ($validation->fails())
        {
    return Redirect::to('fileform')->withErrors($validation)
        ->withInput();
        }
        else
        {
            $file = Input::file('myfile');
            if ($file->move('files', $file
                ->getClientOriginalName()))
            {
                return "Success";
            }
            else
            {
                return "Error";
            }
        }
    });
```

How it works...

We start with a route to hold our form, and then a view for the form's html. At the top of the view, if we get any errors in validation, they will be echoed out here. The form begins with `Form::open (array('files' => TRUE))`, which will set the default action, method, and `enctype` for us.

Next we create a route to capture the post data and validate it. We set a `$rules` variable as an array, first checking for a specific mime type. There can be as few or as many as we want. Then we make sure the file is less than 1000 kilobytes, or 1 megabyte.

If the file isn't valid, we navigate the user back to the form with the error messages. The `$error` variable is automatically created in our view if Laravel detects a flashed error message. If it is valid, we attempt to save the file to the server. If it saves correctly, we'll see `"Success"`, and if not, we'll see `"Error"`.

There's more...

One other common validation for files is to check for an image. For that, we can use this in our `$rules` array:

```
'myfile' => 'image'
```

This will check to make sure the file is either a `.jpg`, `.png`, `.gif`, or `.bmp` file.

▶ The *Creating a file uploader* recipe

Creating a custom error message

Laravel has built-in error messages if a validation fails, but we may want to customize those messages to make our application unique. This recipe shows a few different ways to create custom error messages.

Getting ready

For this recipe, we just need a standard installation of Laravel.

How to do it...

To complete this recipe, follow these steps:

1. Create a route in `routes.php` to hold the form:

```
Route::get('myform', function()
{
    return View::make('myform');
});
```

2. Create a view named `myform.php` and add a form:

```
<h1>User Info</h1>
<?php $messages =  $errors->all
    ('<p style="color:red">:message</p>') ?>
<?php
foreach ($messages as $msg)
{
    echo $msg;
}
?>
<?= Form::open() ?>
<?= Form::label('email', 'Email') ?>
<?= Form::text('email', Input::old('email')) ?>
<br>
<?= Form::label('username', 'Username') ?>
<?= Form::text('username', Input::old('username')) ?>
<br>
<?= Form::label('password', 'Password') ?>
<?= Form::password('password') ?>
<br>
```

```
<?= Form::submit('Send it!') ?>
<?= Form::close() ?>
```

3. Create a route that handles our POST data and validates it:

```
Route::post('myform', array('before' => 'csrf', function()
{
    $rules = array(
        'email'    => 'required|email|min:6',
        'username' => 'required|min:6',
        'password' => 'required'
    );

    $messages = array(
        'min' => 'Way too short! The :attribute must be at
            least :min characters in length.',
        'username.required' => 'We really, really need a
            Username.'
    );

    $validation = Validator::make(Input::all(), $rules,
        $messages);

    if ($validation->fails())
    {
        return Redirect::to('myform')->withErrors
            ($validation)->withInput();
    }

    return Redirect::to('myresults')->withInput();
}));
```

4. Open the file app/lang/en/validation.php, where en is the default language of the app. In our case, we're using English. At the bottom of the file, update the attributes array as the following:

```
'attributes' => array(
    'password' => 'Super Secret Password (shhhh!)'
),
```

5. Create a route to handle a successful form submission:

```
Route::get('myresults', function()
{
    return dd(Input::old());
});
```

How it works...

We first create a fairly simple form, and since we aren't passing any parameters to
`Form::open()`, it will POST the data to the same URL. We then create a route to accept the
POST data and validate it. As a best practice, we're also adding in the `csrf` filter before our
`post` route. This will provide some extra security against cross-site request frogeries.

The first variable we set in our `post` route will hold our rules. The next variable will hold any
custom messages we want to use if there's an error. There are a few different ways to set
the message.

The first message to customize is for `min` size. In this case, it will display the same message
for any validation errors where there's a `min` rule. We can use `:attribute` and `:min` to hold
the form field name and minimum size when the error is displayed.

Our second message is used only for a specific form field and for a specific validation rule. We
put the form field name first, followed by a period, and then the rule. Here, we are checking
whether the username is required and setting the error message.

Our third message is set in the language file for validations. In the `attributes` array, we
can set any of our form field names to display any custom text we'd like. Also, if we decide to
customize a particular error message across the entire application, we can alter the default
message at the top of this file.

There's more...

If we look in the `app/lang` directory, we see quite a few translations that are already part of
Laravel. If our application is localized, we can set custom validation error messages in any
language we choose.

See also

▸   The *Creating a simple form* recipe

Adding a honey pot to a form

A sad reality of the Web is that there are "spam bots" that search the web and look for forms
to submit spam to. One way to help combat this is to use a technique called a **honey pot**. In
this recipe, we'll create a custom validation to check for spam submissions.

Getting ready

For this recipe, we just need a standard Laravel installation.

How to do it...

To complete this recipe, follow these steps:

1. Create a route in `routes.php` to hold our form:

```php
Route::get('myform', function()
{
    return View::make('myapp');
});
```

2. Create a view in our `app/view` directory named as `myform.php` and add the form:

```php
<h1>User Info</h1>
<?php $messages =  $errors->all('<p style =
    "color:red">:message</p>') ?>
<?php
foreach ($messages as $msg)
{
    echo $msg;
}
?>
<?= Form::open() ?>
<?= Form::label('email', 'Email') ?>
<?= Form::text('email', Input::old('email')) ?>
<br>
<?= Form::label('username', 'Username') ?>
<?= Form::text('username', Input::old('username')) ?>
<br>
<?= Form::label('password', 'Password') ?>
<?= Form::password('password') ?>
<?= Form::text('no_email', '', array('style' =>
    'display:none')) ?>
<br>
<?= Form::submit('Send it!') ?>
<?= Form::close() ?>
```

3. Create a route in our `routes.php` file to handle the `post` data, and validate it:

```php
Route::post('myform', array('before' => 'csrf', function()
{
    $rules = array(
        'email'    => 'required|email',
        'password' => 'required',
        'no_email' => 'honey_pot'
    );
    $messages = array(
```

```
            'honey_pot' => 'Nothing should be in this field.'
        );
        $validation = Validator::make(Input::all(), $rules,
            $messages);

        if ($validation->fails())
        {
            return Redirect::to('myform')->withErrors
                ($validation)->withInput();
        }

        return Redirect::to('myresults')->withInput();
    }));
```

4. In our `routes.php` file, create a custom validation:

```
Validator::extend('honey_pot', function($attribute, $value,
    $parameters)
{
    return $value == '';
});
```

5. Create a simple route to use for a success page:

```
Route::get('myresults', function()
{
    return dd(Input::old());
});
```

How it works...

We first create a fairly simple form; since we aren't passing any parameters to `Form::open()`, it will POST the data to the same URL. In the form, we create a field that's designed to be empty, but hide it from the user using CSS. By naming it as something with the word `email` in it, many spam bots will mistake it for an `email` field and try to populate it.

We then create a route to accept the `post` data and validate it, along with having a `csrf` filter added before the route. We add a custom validation rule to our `no_email` field, which will make sure that field stays empty. We also create an error message for that rule in the `$messages` array.

Next, we actually create our custom validation rule in the `routes` file. This rule will get the value from the form field and return TRUE if the value is empty.

Now, if a bot tries to fill in the entire form, it will not validate since that extra field is designed to stay empty.

There's more...

One alternative to creating a custom validation is to use the rule `size: 0`, which will make sure the `honey_pot` field is exactly `0` characters in length. However, this method keeps the validation check much simpler.

We might also want to redirect any honey pot errors to another page that doesn't have a form. That way, any automatic form submission scripts won't continue to try and submit the form.

Uploading an image using Redactor

There are a few different JavaScript libraries that can turn a form's text area into a WYSIWYG editor. Redactor is a newer library but is very well coded and has gained quite a bit of popularity in a short amount of time. For this recipe, we'll apply Redactor to our Laravel form, and create routes to allow for image uploads through Redactor.

Getting ready

We need to download a copy of Redactor from `https://github.com/dybskiy/redactor-js/tree/master/redactor`. Download `redactor.min.js` and save it to the `public/js` directory. Download `redactor.css` and save it to the `public/css` directory.

How to do it...

To complete this recipe, follow these steps:

1. Create a route in our `routes.php` file to hold our form with the `redactor` field:

```
Route::get('redactor', function()
{
    return View::make('redactor');
});
```

2. Create a view in our `app/views` directory and name it as `redactor.php`:

```
<!DOCTYPE html>
<html>
    <head>
        <title>Laravel and Redactor</title>
        <meta charset="utf-8">
        <link rel="stylesheet" href="css/redactor.css" />
        <script src="//ajax.googleapis.com/ajax/libs/
            jquery/1.10.2/jquery.min.js"></script>
        <script src="js/redactor.min.js"></script>
    </head>
```

```
<body>
    <?= Form::open() ?>
    <?= Form::label('mytext', 'My Text') ?>
    <br>
    <?= Form::textarea('mytext', '', array('id' =>
        'mytext')) ?>
    <br>
    <?= Form::submit('Send it!') ?>
    <?= Form::close() ?>
    <script type="text/javascript">
        $(function() {
            $('#mytext').redactor({
                imageUpload: 'redactorupload'
            });
        });
    </script>
</body>
</html>
```

3. Make a route that will handle the image upload:

```
Route::post('redactorupload', function()
{
    $rules = array(
        'file' => 'image|max:10000'
    );
    $validation = Validator::make(Input::all(), $rules);
    $file = Input::file('file');
    if ($validation->fails())
    {
        return FALSE;
    }
    else
    {
        if ($file->move('files', $file->
            getClientOriginalName()))
        {
            return Response::json(array('filelink' =>
                'files/' . $file->getClientOriginalName()));
        }
        else
        {
            return FALSE;
        }
    }
});
```

4. Create another route to show our form input after it's submitted:

```
Route::post('redactor', function()
{
    return dd(Input::all());
});
```

How it works...

After creating our form route, we create the view to hold our form HTML. In the head of the page, we load in the redactor CSS, the jquery library (using Google's CDN), and the redactor JavaScript file.

Our form will only have one field, a text area named `mytext`. In our script area, we initialize Redactor on the text area field and set the `imageUpload` parameter to a route or controller that will accept the image upload. Ours is set to `redactorupload`, so we create a route for it that accepts `post` data.

In our `redactorupload` route, we do some validation and, if everything is okay, the image will upload to our images directory. To get the image to display in our text area, it needs a JSON array with a file link as the key and the image path as the value. For this, we'll use Laravel's built-in `Response::json` method, and pass in an array with the image's location.

On our form page, if the image validated and uploaded correctly, Redactor will display the image inside the text area. If we submit, we'll see the text included the `<img>` tag and the image path.

There's more...

While this recipe is specifically for image uploads, non-image file uploads work in a very similar manner. The only real difference is that file upload route should also return filename in the JSON output.

Cropping an image with Jcrop

Image editing and manipulation can sometimes be a difficult thing to implement in our application. Using Laravel and the Jcrop JavaScript library, we can make the task much simpler.

Getting ready

We need to download the Jcrop library from `http://deepliquid.com/content/Jcrop_Download.html` and unzip it. Put the file `jquery.Jcrop.min.js` into our `public/js` directory, and the `jquery.Jcrop.min.css` and `Jcrop.gif` files into our `public/css` directory. We'll use the Google CDN version of jQuery. We also need to make sure we have the GD library installed on our server, so we can do image manipulation. In our `public` directory, we'll need an images folder to store the images, and should have the permission set for it to be writable.

How to do it...

Follow these steps to finish this recipe:

1. Let's create a route in our `routes.php` file to hold our form:

```
Route::get('imageform', function()
{
    return View::make('imageform');
});
```

2. Create the form for uploading an image, in `app/views` with the filename `imageform.php`:

```
<h1>Laravel and Jcrop</h1>
<?= Form::open(array('files' => true)) ?>
<?= Form::label('image', 'My Image') ?>
<br>
<?= Form::file('image') ?>
<br>
<?= Form::submit('Upload!') ?>
<?= Form::close() ?>
```

3. Make a route to handle the image upload and validation:

```
Route::post('imageform', function()
{
    $rules = array(
        'image' => 'required|mimes:jpeg,jpg|max:10000'
    );

    $validation = Validator::make(Input::all(), $rules);

    if ($validation->fails())
    {
        return Redirect::to('imageform')->withErrors
            ($validation);
    }
```

```
        else
        {
            $file = Input::file('image');
            $file_name = $file->getClientOriginalName();
            if ($file->move('images', $file_name))
            {
                return Redirect::to('jcrop')->with('image',
                    $file_name);
            }
            else
            {
                return "Error uploading file";
            }
        }
    }
});
```

4. Create a route for our Jcrop form:

```
Route::get('jcrop', function()
{
    return View::make('jcrop')->with('image', 'images/'
        . Session::get('image'));
});
```

5. Make a form, where we can crop the image, in our `app/views` directory with the filename `jcrop.php`:

```html
<html>
    <head>
        <title>Laravel and Jcrop</title>
        <meta charset="utf-8">
        <link rel="stylesheet" href="css/
            jquery.Jcrop.min.css" />
        <script src="//ajax.googleapis.com/ajax/libs/
            jquery/1.10.2/jquery.min.js"></script>
        <script src="js/jquery.Jcrop.min.js"></script>
    </head>
    <body>
        <h2>Image Cropping with Laravel and Jcrop</h2>
        <img src="<?php echo $image ?>" id="cropimage">

        <?= Form::open() ?>
        <?= Form::hidden('image', $image) ?>
        <?= Form::hidden('x', '', array('id' => 'x')) ?>
        <?= Form::hidden('y', '', array('id' => 'y')) ?>
        <?= Form::hidden('w', '', array('id' => 'w')) ?>
        <?= Form::hidden('h', '', array('id' => 'h')) ?>
        <?= Form::submit('Crop it!') ?>
```

```
        <?= Form::close() ?>

        <script type="text/javascript">
            $(function() {
                $('#cropimage').Jcrop({
                    onSelect: updateCoords
                });
            });
            function updateCoords(c) {
                $('#x').val(c.x);
                $('#y').val(c.y);
                $('#w').val(c.w);
                $('#h').val(c.h);
            };
        </script>
    </body>
</html>
```

6. Create a route that will process the image and display it:

```
Route::post('jcrop', function()
{
    $quality = 90;

    $src  = Input::get('image');
    $img  = imagecreatefromjpeg($src);
    $dest = ImageCreateTrueColor(Input::get('w'),
        Input::get('h'));

    imagecopyresampled($dest, $img, 0, 0, Input::get('x'),
        Input::get('y'), Input::get('w'), Input::get('h'),
        Input::get('w'), Input::get('h'));
    imagejpeg($dest, $src, $quality);

    return "<img src='" . $src . "'>";
});
```

How it works...

We start with a basic file upload; to make it easier, we'll only be using .jpg files. We use the validation to check for the image type as well as making sure the file size is under 10,000 kilobytes. After the file is uploaded, we send the path to our Jcrop route.

In the HTML for the Jcrop route, we create a form with hidden fields that will hold the dimensions of the cropping. The JavaScript function updateCoords takes the cropping dimensions and updates the values of those hidden fields.

When we're done cropping, we submit the form and our route gets the POST data. The image is run through the GD library and cropped, based on the dimensions that were posted. We then overwrite the image and display the updated and cropped file.

There's more...

While this recipe only covers cropping a jpg image, adding in `gif` and `png` images wouldn't be very difficult. We'd just need to get the file extension by passing the file name to Laravel using `File::extension()`. Then, we could either do a `switch` or `if` statement to use the appropriate PHP function. For example, if the extension is `.png`, we'd use `imagecreatefrompng()` and `imagepng()`. More information can be found at `http://www.php.net/manual/en/ref.image.php`.

Creating an autocomplete text input

On our web forms, there may be times when we want to have an autocomplete text field. This can be handy for populating common search terms or product names. Using the jQueryUI Autocomplete library along with Laravel, that becomes an easy task.

Getting ready

In this recipe, we'll be using the CDN versions of jQuery and jQueryUI; however, we could also download them and place them in our `public/js` directory, if we wanted to have them locally.

How to do it...

To complete this recipe, follow these steps:

1. Create a route to hold our autocomplete form:

```
Route::get('autocomplete', function()
{
    return View::make('autocomplete');
});
```

2. Make a view in the `app/views` directory named `autocomplete.php` with our form's HTML and JavaScript:

```
<!DOCTYPE html>
<html>
    <head>
        <title>Laravel Autocomplete</title>
        <meta charset="utf-8">
        <link rel="stylesheet"
            href="//codeorigin.jquery.com/ui/1.10.2/themes/
            smoothness/jquery-ui.css" />
```

```
    <script src="//ajax.googleapis.com/ajax/
        libs/jquery/1.10.2/jquery.min.js"></script>
    <script src="//codeorigin.jquery.com/ui/1.10.2/
        jquery-ui.min.js"></script>
</head>
<body>
    <h2>Laravel Autocomplete</h2>

    <?= Form::open() ?>
    <?= Form::label('auto', 'Find a color: ') ?>
    <?= Form::text('auto', '', array('id' => 'auto'))
        ?>
    <br>
    <?= Form::label('response', 'Our color key: ') ?>
    <?= Form::text('response', '', array('id' =>
        'response', 'disabled' => 'disabled')) ?>
    <?= Form::close() ?>

    <script type="text/javascript">
        $(function() {
            $("#auto").autocomplete({
                source: "getdata",
                minLength: 1,
                select: function( event, ui ) {
                    $('#response').val(ui.item.id);
                }
            });
        });
    </script>
</body>
</html>
```

3. Create a route that will populate the data for the `autocomplete` field:

```
Route::get('getdata', function()
{
    $term = Str::lower(Input::get('term'));
    $data = array(
        'R' => 'Red',
        'O' => 'Orange',
        'Y' => 'Yellow',
        'G' => 'Green',
        'B' => 'Blue',
        'I' => 'Indigo',
        'V' => 'Violet',
    );
```

```
    $return_array = array();

    foreach ($data as $k => $v) {
        if (strpos(Str::lower($v), $term) !== FALSE) {
            $return_array[] = array('value' => $v, 'id' =>
                $k);
        }
    }
    return Response::json($return_array);
});
```

How it works...

In our form, we're creating a text field to accept user input that will be used for the
`autocomplete`. There's also a disabled text field that we can use to see the ID of the value
that was selected. This can be useful if you have an ID for a particular value that's numeric, or
otherwise not named in a standard way. In our example, we're using the first letter of the color
as the ID:

As the user starts typing, `autocomplete` sends a `GET` request to the source that we added,
using the word `term` in the query string. To process this, we create a route that gets the input,
and convert it to lower-case. For our data, we're using a simple array of values but it would be
fairly easy to add in a database query at this point. Our route checks the values in the array to
see if there are any matches with the user input and, if so, adds the ID and value to the array
we will return. Then, we output the array as JSON, for the `autocomplete` script.

Back on our form page, when the user selects a value, we add the ID to the disabled
response field. Many times, this will be a hidden field, which we can then pass on when
we submit the form.

There's more...

If we'd like to have our `getdata` route only accessible from our autocomplete form, or some
other AJAX request, we could simply wrap the code in `if (Request::ajax()) {}` or create
a filter that rejects any non-AJAX requests.

Making a CAPTCHA-style spam catcher

One way to combat "bots" that automatically fill in web forms is by using the CAPTCHA
technique. This shows the user an image with some random letters; the user must fill in a text
field with those letters. In this recipe, we will create a CAPTCHA image and verify that the user
has entered it correctly.

Getting ready

We need a standard Laravel installation and make sure we have the GD2 library installed on our server, so we can create an image.

How to do it...

To complete this recipe, follow these steps:

1. In our app directory, create a directory named `libraries`, and in our `composer.json` file, update it as follows:

```
"autoload": {
    "classmap": [
        "app/commands",
        "app/controllers",
        "app/models",
        "app/database/migrations",
        "app/database/seeds",
        "app/tests/TestCase.php",
        "app/libraries"
    ]
},
```

2. In our `app/libraries` directory, create a file named `Captcha.php` to hold our simple `Captcha` class:

```php
<?php
class Captcha {
    public function make()
    {
        $string = Str::random(6, 'alpha');
        Session::put('my_captcha', $string);

        $width      = 100;
        $height     = 25;
        $image      = imagecreatetruecolor($width,
            $height);
        $text_color = imagecolorallocate($image, 130, 130,
            130);
        $bg_color   = imagecolorallocate($image, 190, 190,
            190);

        imagefilledrectangle($image, 0, 0, $width, $height,
            $bg_color);
```

```
        imagestring($image, 5, 16, 4, $string,
            $text_color);

        ob_start();
        imagejpeg($image);
        $jpg = ob_get_clean();
        return "data:image/jpeg;base64,"
            . base64_encode($jpg);

    }
}
```

3. In the root of our app, open the command-line interface to update the `composer` autoloader:

    php composer.phar dump-autoload

4. Create a route in `routes.php` to hold the form with `captcha`:

    ```
    Route::get('captcha', function()
    {
        $captcha = new Captcha;
        $cap = $captcha->make();
        return View::make('captcha')->with('cap', $cap);
    });
    ```

5. Create our `captcha` view in the `app/views` directory with the name `captcha.php`:

    ```
    <h1>Laravel Captcha</h1>
    <?php
    if (Session::get('captcha_result')) {
        echo '<h2>' . Session::get('captcha_result') . '</h2>';
    }
    ?>
    <?php echo Form::open() ?>
    <?php echo Form::label('captcha', 'Type these letters:') ?>
    <br>
    <img src="<?php echo $cap ?>">
    <br>
    <?php echo Form::text('captcha') ?>
    <br>
    <?php echo Form::submit('Verify!') ?>
    <?php echo Form::close() ?>
    ```

6. Create a route to compare the `captcha` value and the user input:

```
Route::post('captcha', function()
{
    if (Session::get('my_captcha') !==
        Input::get('captcha')) {
        Session::flash('captcha_result', 'No Match.');
    } else {
        Session::flash('captcha_result', 'They Match!');
    }
    return Redirect::to('captcha');
});
```

How it works...

We begin by updating our `composer.json` file to add our `libraries` directory to the autoloader. Now, we can add any classes or libraries we'd like into that directory, even if they're custom classes or possibly some legacy code.

To keep things simple, we create a simple `Captcha` class with a single `make()` method. In this method, we first create a random string using Laravel's `Str:random()`, which we tell to output a 6-character string of only letters. We then save that string to a session, so we can use it for validation later.

Using the string, we create a 100x25 pixel jpg image, with a gray background and darker gray text. Instead of saving the file to the server, we use the output buffer and save the image data to a variable. That way, we can create a data URI to send back to our route.

Next, we need to run composer's `dump-autoload` command, so our new class can be used by the application.

In our `captcha` route, we use the `Captcha` class to create the `captcha` data URI and send it to our form. For our purposes, the form will simply display the image and ask for the characters in a text field.

When the user submits the form, we compare the Session that the `Captcha` class created with the user input. In this recipe, we're just checking if the two values match but we could also create a custom validation method and add it our rules. We then set a session saying if it matched or not, and return the user back to the CAPTCHA page.

3
Authenticating Your Application

In this chapter, we will cover:

- ▸ Setting up and configuring the Auth library
- ▸ Creating an authentication system
- ▸ Retrieving and updating user info after logging in
- ▸ Restricting access to certain pages
- ▸ Setting up OAuth with the HybridAuth package
- ▸ Using OpenID for logins
- ▸ Logging in using Facebook credentials
- ▸ Logging in using Twitter credentials
- ▸ Logging in using LinkedIn

Introduction

Many modern web applications include some way for users to register and log in. To make sure our application and our users' information is secure, we need to make sure that each user is properly authenticated. Laravel includes a great `Auth` class that makes this task very easy to accomplish. In this chapter, we'll begin with setting up our own authentication system, and move on to using third-party authentication in our Laravel app.

Setting up and configuring the Auth library

To use Laravel's authentication system, we need to make sure it's set up correctly. In this recipe, we'll see a common way to accomplish the setup.

Getting ready

To set up the authentication, we just need to have Laravel installed and a MySQL instance running.

How to do it...

To complete this recipe, follow these steps:

1. Go into your `app/config/session.php` config file and make sure it's set to use `native`:

   ```
   'driver' => 'native'
   ```

2. The `app/config/auth.php` config file defaults should be fine but make sure they are set as follows:

   ```
   'driver' => 'eloquent',
   'model' => 'User',
   'table' => 'users',
   ```

3. In MySQL, create a database named as `authapp` and make sure the settings are correct in the `app/config/database.php` config file. The following are the settings that we'll be using:

   ```
   'default' => 'mysql',

   'connections' => array(

       'mysql' => array(
           'driver'    => 'mysql',
           'host'      => 'localhost',
           'database'  => 'authapp',
           'username'  => 'root',
           'password'  => '',
           'charset'   => 'utf8',
           'prefix'    => '',
       ),
   ),
   ```

4. We'll set up our `Users` table using migrations and the Schema builder with the Artisan command line, so we need to create our migrations table:

   ```
   php artisan migrate:install
   ```

5. Create the migration for our `Users` table:

```
php artisan migrate:make create_users_table
```

6. In the `app/database/migrations` directory, there will be a new file that has the date followed by `create_users_table.php` as the filename. In that file, we create our table:

```php
<?php

use Illuminate\Database\Migrations\Migration;

class CreateUsersTable extends Migration {

    /**
     * Run the migrations.
     *
     * @return void
     */
    public function up()
    {
        Schema::create('users', function($table)
        {
            $table->increments('id');
            $table->string('email');
            $table->string('password', 64);
            $table->string('name');
            $table->boolean('admin');
            $table->timestamps();
        });

    }

    /**
     * Reverse the migrations.
     *
     * @return void
     */
    public function down()
    {
        Schema::drop('users');
    }

}
```

7. Run the migration in Artisan to create our table and everything should be set up:

```
php artisan migrate
```

How it works...

Authentication uses sessions to store user information, so we first need to make sure our Sessions are configured correctly. There are various ways to store sessions, including using the database or Redis, but for our purpose we'll just use the `native` driver, which leverages Symfony's native session driver.

When setting up the auth configuration, we'll be using the Eloquent ORM as our driver, an e-mail address as our username, and the model will be User. Laravel ships with a default User model and it works very well out of the box, so we'll use it. For the sake of simplicity, we'll stick with the default configuration of the table name, a pluralized version of the model class name, but we could customize it if we wanted.

Once we make sure our database configuration is set, we can use Artisan to create our migrations. In our migration, we'll create our user's table, and store the e-mail address, password, a name, and a boolean field to store whether the user is an admin or not. Once that's complete, we run the migration, and our database will be set up to build our authentication system.

Creating an authentication system

In this recipe, we'll be creating a simple authentication system. It can be used as it is or extended to include much more functionality.

Getting ready

We will be using the code created in the *Setting up and configuring the Auth library* recipe as the basis for our authentication system.

How to do it...

To finish this recipe, follow these steps:

1. Create a route in our `routes.php` file to hold our registration form:

    ```
    Route::get('registration', function()
    {
        return View::make('registration');
    });
    ```

2. Create a registration form by creating a new file in `app/views` named as `registration.php`:

    ```
    <!DOCTYPE html>
    <html>
        <head>
    ```

```
        <title>Laravel Authentication - Registration
        </title>
        <meta charset="utf-8">
    </head>
    <body>
        <h2>Laravel Authentication - Registration</h2>
        <?php $messages = $errors->all('<p style=
            "color:red">:message</p>') ?>
        <?php foreach ($messages as $msg): ?>
            <?= $msg ?>
        <?php endforeach; ?>


<?= Form::open() ?>
        <?= Form::label('email', 'Email address: ') ?>
        <?= Form::text('email', Input::old('email')) ?>
        <br>
        <?= Form::label('password', 'Password: ') ?>
        <?= Form::password('password') ?>
        <br>
        <?= Form::label('password_confirm',
            'Retype Password: ') ?>
        <?= Form::password('password_confirm') ?>
        <br>
        <?= Form::label('name', 'Name: ') ?>
        <?= Form::text('name', Input::old('name')) ?>
        <br>
        <?= Form::label('admin', 'Admin?: ') ?>
        <?= Form::checkbox('admin','true',
            Input::old('admin')) ?>
        <br>
        <?= Form::submit('Register!') ?>
        <?= Form::close() ?>
    </body>
</html>
```

3. Make a route to process the registration page:

```
Route::post('registration', array('before' => 'csrf',
    function()
{
    $rules = array(
        'email'    => 'required|email|unique:users',
        'password' => 'required|same:password_confirm',
        'name'     => 'required'
    );
```

```
    $validation = Validator::make(Input::all(), $rules);

    if ($validation->fails())
    {
        return Redirect::to('registration')->withErrors
            ($validation)->withInput();
    }

    $user           = new User;
    $user->email    = Input::get('email');
    $user->password = Hash::make(Input::get('password'));
    $user->name     = Input::get('name');
    $user->admin    = Input::get('admin') ? 1 : 0;
    if ($user->save())
    {
        Auth::loginUsingId($user->id);
        return Redirect::to('profile');
    }
    return Redirect::to('registration')->withInput();
}));
```

4. Make a simple page for your profile by adding a route in `routes.php`:

```
Route::get('profile', function()
{
    if (Auth::check())
    {
        return 'Welcome! You have been authorized!';
    }
    else
    {
        return 'Please <a href="login">Login</a>';
    }
});
```

5. Create a login route in `routes.php` to hold the login form:

```
Route::get('login', function()
{
    return View::make('login');
});
```

6. In our `app/views` directory, create a file named `login.php`:

```
<!DOCTYPE html>
<html>
    <head>
```

```
        <title>Laravel Authentication - Login</title>
        <meta charset="utf-8">
    </head>
    <body>
        <h2>Laravel Authentication - Login</h2>
        <?= '<span style="color:red">' .
            Session::get('login_error') . '</span>' ?>

        <?= Form::open() ?>
        <?= Form::label('email', 'Email address: ') ?>
        <?= Form::text('email', Input::old('email')) ?>
        <br>
        <?= Form::label('password', 'Password: ') ?>
        <?= Form::password('password') ?>
        <br>
        <?= Form::submit('Login!') ?>
        <?= Form::close() ?>
    </body>
</html>
```

7. Create a route in `routes.php` to authenticate the login:

```
Route::post('login', function()
{
    $user = array(
        'username' => Input::get('email'),
        'password' => Input::get('password')
    );

    if (Auth::attempt($user))
    {
        return Redirect::to('profile');
    }

    return Redirect::to('login')->with('login_error',
        'Could not log in.');
});
```

8. Create a route in `routes.php` that is a secured page:

```
Route::get('secured', array('before' => 'auth', function()
{
    return 'This is a secured page!';
})));
```

How it works...

To begin with, we create a fairly simple registration system. In our registration form, we'll be asking for an e-mail address, password, password confirmation, a name, and then an option for whether the user is an admin. In the form fields, we also add `Input::old()`; thus, if the form doesn't validate correctly, we can repopulate the fields without needing the user to re-enter all the information.

Our form then posts, adding in the CSRF filter, and runs through some validation. If the validation passes, we create a new instance of our User model and add in the fields from our form. For the password, we use `Hash::make()` to keep the password secure. Since our admin field accepts a boolean value, we see if the admin checkbox was checked; if so, we set the value to 1.

If everything is saved correctly, we can automatically log in the user by passing the just created user ID to `Auth::loginUsingId()`, and redirect them to the profile page.

The first thing the profile route does is run `Auth::check()` to see if the user is actually logged in. If he/she isn't, it will display a link to the login page.

The login page is a simple form asking for e-mail ID and password. When submitted, we put those two values in an array and pass them to `Auth::attempt()`, which will automatically hash our password, and look up the credentials in the database. If it's successful, the `Auth` class will set a session and we redirect the user to the profile page.

If the user happens to try and access the *secured* routes, the system will direct them to the login page. Using Laravel's `Redirect::intended()`, we can then direct them back to the page they originally tried to access.

See also

▶   The *Setting up and configuring the Auth library* recipe

Retrieving and updating user info after logging in

After a user is logged in, we will need to get the information we have about him/her. In this recipe, we'll see how to get that information.

Getting ready

We will be using the code created in the *Setting up and configuring the Auth library* and *Creating an authentication system* recipes as the basis for this recipe.

How to do it...

To complete this recipe, follow these steps:

1. Update the profile route with this code:

```
Route::get('profile', function()
{
    if (Auth::check())
    {
        return View::make('profile')->with('user',
            Auth::user());
    }
    else
    {
        return Redirect::to('login')->with('login_error',
            'You must login first.');
    }
});
```

2. Create our profile view in the `app/views` directory by creating a file named as `profile.php`:

```
<?php echo Session::get('notify') ?  "<p style='color:
    green'>" . Session::get('notify') . "</p>" : "" ?>
<h1>Welcome <?php echo $user->name ?></h1>
<p>Your email: <?php echo $user->email ?></p>
<p>Your account was created on: <?php echo $user
    ->created_at ?></p>
<p><a href="<?= URL::to('profile-edit') ?>">Edit your
    information</a></p>
```

3. Make a route to hold our form to edit the information:

```
Route::get('profile-edit', function()
{
    if (Auth::check())
    {
        $user = Input::old() ? (object) Input::old() :
            Auth::user();
        return View::make('profile_edit')->with('user',
            $user);
    }
});
```

4. Create a view for our edit form:

```
<h2>Edit User Info</h2>
<?php $messages =   $errors->all('<p style="color:
    red">:message</p>') ?>
<?php foreach ($messages as $msg): ?>
    <?= $msg ?>
<?php endforeach; ?>
<?= Form::open() ?>
<?= Form::label('email', 'Email address: ') ?>
<?= Form::text('email', $user->email) ?>
<br>
<?= Form::label('password', 'Password: ') ?>
<?= Form::password('password') ?>
<br>
<?= Form::label('password_confirm', 'Retype Password: ') ?>
<?= Form::password('password_confirm') ?>
<br>
<?= Form::label('name', 'Name: ') ?>
<?= Form::text('name',   $user->name) ?>
<br>
<?= Form::submit('Update!') ?>
<?= Form::close() ?>
```

5. Make a route to process the form:

```
Route::post('profile-edit', function()
{
    $rules = array(
        'email'    => 'required|email',
        'password' => 'same:password_confirm',
        'name'     => 'required'
    );
    $validation = Validator::make(Input::all(), $rules);

    if ($validation->fails())
    {
        return Redirect::to('profile-edit')->withErrors
            ($validation)->withInput();
    }

    $user = User::find(Auth::user()->id);
    $user->email = Input::get('email');
    if (Input::get('password')) {
        $user->password = Hash::make
            (Input::get('password'));
```

```
    }
    $user->name = Input::get('name');
    if ($user->save())
    {
        return Redirect::to('profile')->with('notify',
            'Information updated');
    }
    return Redirect::to('profile-edit')->withInput();
});
```

How it works...

To get our user's information and allow him/her to update it, we start by reworking on our profile route. We create a profile view and pass `Auth::user()` to it in the variable `$user`. Then, in the view file, we simply echo out any of the information we collected. We're also creating a link to a page where the user can edit his/her information.

Our profile edit page first checks to make sure the user is logged in. If so, we want to populate the `$user` variable. Since we'll redisplay the form if there is a validation error, we first check if there's anything in `Input::old()`. If not, this is probably a new visit to the page, so we just use `Auth::user()`. If `Input::old()` is being used, we'll recast it as an object, since it's normally an array, and use that in our `$user` variable.

Our edit view form is very similar to our registration form, except that, if we're logged in, the form is already populated.

When the form is submitted, it is run through some validation. If everything is valid, we need to get the User from the database, using `User::find()` and the user ID that's stored in `Auth::user()`. We then add our form input to the user object. With the password field, if it was left empty, we can assume that the user didn't want to change it. So we'll only update the password if something was already entered.

Finally, we save the user information and redirect him/her back to the profile page.

There's more...

The e-mail value in our database will probably need to be unique. For this recipe, we might want to do a quick check of the user's table, and make sure the e-mail address being updated isn't used somewhere else.

See also

> ▸ The *Creating an authentication system* recipe

Restricting access to certain pages

In this recipe, we'll explore how to restrict access to various pages in our app. This way, we can make pages viewable to only those with the correct credentials.

Getting ready

We will be using the code created in the *Setting up and configuring the Auth library* and *Creating an authentication system* recipes as the basis for this recipe.

How to do it...

To complete this recipe, follow these steps:

1. Create a filter in our `filters.php` file that checks for logged-in users. The default Laravel `auth` filter will be fine:

```
Route::filter('auth', function()
{
    if (Auth::guest()) return Redirect::guest('login');
});
```

2. Create a filter in `filter.php` for checking if a user is an admin:

```
Route::filter('auth_admin', function()
{
    if (Auth::guest()) return Redirect::guest('login');
    if (Auth::user()->admin != TRUE)
        return Redirect::to('restricted');
});
```

3. Make a route that we restrict to logged-in users:

```
Route::get('restricted', array('before' => 'auth',
    function()
{
    return 'This page is restricted to logged-in users!
        <a href="admin">Admins Click Here.</a>';
}));
```

4. Make a route that is restricted to admins:

```
Route::get('admin', array('before' => 'auth_admin',
    function()
{
    return 'This page is restricted to Admins only!';
}));
```

How it works...

Filters are a powerful part of Laravel and can be used to simplify many tasks. The default `auth` filter that comes with Laravel simply checks if a user is logged in or not and, if not, redirects him/her to the login page. In our `restricted` route, we add the `auth` filter to run before the function is executed.

Our `auth_admin` filter checks to make sure the user is logged in and also checks if the user is set as `admin`. If not, he/she is redirected back to the normal restricted page.

Setting up OAuth with the HybridAuth package

There may be times when we don't want to worry about storing users' passwords. In that case, OAuth has become a popular alternative that allows us to authenticate a user based on a third-party service such as Facebook or Twitter. This recipe will show how to set up the `HybridAuth` package to make OAuth easy.

Getting ready

For this recipe, we need a standard Laravel installation and a way to access the command-line interface, so we can use the Artisan command-line utility.

How to do it...

To complete this recipe, follow these steps:

1. Open our app's `composer.json` file and add HybridAuth to the `require` section, so it should look like this:

```
"require": {
    "laravel/framework": "4.0.*",
    "hybridauth/hybridauth": "dev-master"
},
```

2. In the command-line interface, update composer as follows:

```
php composer.phar update
```

3. In the `app/config` directory, create a new file named as `oauth.php`:

```
<?php
return array(
    "base_url"   => "http://path/to/our/app/oauth/auth",
    "providers"  => array (
```

```
                "OpenID" => array ("enabled" => true),
                "Facebook" => array (
                    "enabled"   => TRUE,
                    "keys"      => array ("id" => "APP_ID", "secret"
                        => "APP_SECRET"),
                    "scope"     => "email",
                ),
                "Twitter" => array (
                    "enabled" => true,
                    "keys"     => array ("key" => "CONSUMER_KEY",
                        "secret" => "CONSUMER_SECRET")
                ),
                "LinkedIn" => array (
                    "enabled" => true,
                    "keys" => array ("key" => "APP_KEY", "secret"
                        => "APP_SECRET")
                )
            )
        )
    );
```

How it works...

We begin by adding the HybridAuth package to our composer files. Now, when we update composer, it will automatically download the package and install it for us. From then on, we can use the library throughout our app.

Our next step is to set up a configuration file. This file begins with a URL to which the authentication site will send the user back. That URL should be routed to either a route or controller where we'll run HybridAuth and do the actual authentication. Finally, we need to add in our credentials for the sites we want to authenticate against. A full list of sites can be found at the HybridAuth site: http://hybridauth.sourceforge.net/userguide.html.

Using OpenID for logins

If we don't want to store our users' passwords in our application, there are other authentication methods that use third parties, such as OAuth and OpenID. In this recipe, we'll use OpenID to log in our users.

Getting ready

For this recipe, we need to have a standard installation of Laravel and complete the *Setting up OAuth with the HybridAuth package* recipe.

How to do it...

To complete this recipe, follow these steps:

1. In our `app/config` directory, create a new file named as `openid_auth.php`:

```php
<?php
return array(
    "base_url"  => "http://path/to/our/app/openid/auth",
    "providers" => array (
        "OpenID" => array ("enabled" => TRUE)
    )
);
```

2. In our `routes.php` file, create a route to hold our login form:

```php
Route::get('login', function()
{
    return View::make('login');
});
```

3. In our `app/views` directory, create a new view named as `login.php`:

```php
<!DOCTYPE html>
<html>
    <head>
        <title>Laravel Open ID Login</title>
        <meta charset="utf-8">
    </head>
    <body>
        <h1>OpenID Login</h1>
        <?= Form::open(array('url' => 'openid', 'method' =>
            'POST')) ?>
        <?= Form::label('openid_identity', 'OpenID') ?>
        <?= Form::text('openid_identity', Input::old
            ('openid_identity')) ?>
        <br>
        <?= Form::submit('Log In!') ?>
        <?= Form::close() ?>
    </body>
</html>
```

4. In `routes.php`, create the route to run the authentication:

```php
Route::any('openid/{auth?}', function($auth = NULL)
{
    if ($auth == 'auth') {
        try {
```

```
            Hybrid_Endpoint::process();
        } catch (Exception $e) {
            return Redirect::to('openid');
        }
        return;
    }

    try {
        $oauth = new Hybrid_Auth(app_path()
            . '/config/openid_auth.php');
        $provider = $oauth->authenticate('OpenID',
            array('openid_identifier' =>
            Input::get('openid_identity')));
        $profile = $provider->getUserProfile();
    }
    catch(Exception $e) {
        return $e->getMessage();
    }
    echo 'Welcome ' . $profile->firstName . ' ' . $profile
        ->lastName . '<br>';
    echo 'Your email: ' . $profile->email . '<br>';
    dd($profile);
});
```

How it works...

We start by creating a config file for the HybridAuth library, setting the URL where the user will be redirected after authentication, and enabling OpenID.

Next, we create route and a view where the user can enter the OpenID URL they want to use. A popular one is that of Google, so we suggest using the URL `https://www.google.com/accounts/o8/id` or even have it automatically set as a value in the form.

After submitting the form, we should be directed to the authentication system of the OpenID site and then redirected back to our site. There, we can show the user's name, and e-mail ID, and show all the information that was sent back.

There's more...

Much more information about what OpenID offers is available at `http://openid.net/developers/specs/`.

Logging in using Facebook credentials

If we don't want to worry about storing a user's information and credentials, we could use OAuth to authenticate with another service. One of the most popular is using Facebook for logins. With Laravel and the HybridAuth library, we can easily implement OAuth authentication with Facebook.

Getting ready

For this recipe, we need to have the HybridAuth package installed and set up as in the *Setting up OAuth with the HybridAuth package* recipe.

How to do it...

To complete this recipe, follow these steps:

1. Create a new App at `https://developers.facebook.com`.

2. Get the App ID and App Secret keys, and in the `app/config` directory, create a file named as `fb_auth.php`:

```php
<?php
return array(
    "base_url" => "http://path/to/our/app/fbauth/auth",
    "providers" => array (
        "Facebook" => array (
            "enabled"   => TRUE,
            "keys" => array ("id" => "APP_ID", "secret" =>
                "APP_SECRET"),
            "scope" => "email"
        )
    )
);
```

3. Create a route in `routes.php` to hold our Facebook login button:

```php
Route::get('facebook', function()
{
    return "<a href='fbauth'>Login with Facebook</a>";
});
```

4. Make a route to process the login information and display it:

```php
Route::get('fbauth/{auth?}', function($auth = NULL)
{
    if ($auth == 'auth') {
        try {
```

```
            Hybrid_Endpoint::process();
        } catch (Exception $e) {
            return Redirect::to('fbauth');
        }
        return;
    }

    try {
        $oauth = new Hybrid_Auth(app_path()
            . '/config/fb_auth.php');
        $provider = $oauth->authenticate('Facebook');
        $profile = $provider->getUserProfile();
    }
    catch(Exception $e) {
        return $e->getMessage();
    }
    echo 'Welcome ' . $profile->firstName . ' '
        . $profile->lastName . '<br>';
    echo 'Your email: ' . $profile->email . '<br>';
    dd($profile);
});
```

How it works...

After getting our Facebook API credentials, we need to create a configuration file with those credentials and our callback URL. We also need to pass in the scope, which is any extra permission we might want from our user. In this case, we're just going to get their e-mail ID.

Our facebook login page is a simple link to a route where we do the authentication. The user will then be taken to Facebook to login and/or authorize our site, and then redirected back to our `fbauth` route.

At this point, we're just displaying the information that was returned, but we'd also probably want to save the information to our own database.

There's more...

If we're testing this on our local computer using something like MAMP or WAMP, Facebook allows us to use the callback URL of localhost.

Logging in using Twitter credentials

If we don't want to worry about storing the user's information and credentials, we could use OAuth to authenticate with another service. A popular service to use for logins is Twitter. With Laravel and the HybridAuth library, we can easily implement OAuth authentication with Twitter.

Getting ready

For this recipe, we need to have the HybridAuth package installed and set up as in the *Setting up OAuth with the HybridAuth package* recipe.

How to do it...

To complete this recipe, follow these steps:

1. Create a new app at `https://dev.twitter.com/apps`.

2. Get the Consumer Key and the Consumer Secret, and in the `app/config` directory, create a file named as `tw_auth.php`:

```php
<?php
return array(
    "base_url"  => "http://path/to/our/app/twauth/auth",
    "providers" => array (
        "Twitter" => array (
            "enabled" => true,
            "keys"    => array ("key" => "CONSUMER_KEY",
                "secret" => "CONSUMER_SECRET")
        )
    )
);
```

3. Create a route in `routes.php` for our Twitter login button:

```php
Route::get('twitter', function()
{
    return "<a href='twauth'>Login with Twitter</a>";
});
```

4. Make a route to process the Twitter information:

```php
Route::get('twauth/{auth?}', function($auth = NULL)
{
    if ($auth == 'auth') {
        try {
            Hybrid_Endpoint::process();
        } catch (Exception $e) {
```

```
                 return Redirect::to('twauth');
             }
             return;
        }

        try {
             $oauth = new Hybrid_Auth(app_path()
                  . '/config/tw_auth.php');
             $provider = $oauth->authenticate('Twitter');
             $profile = $provider->getUserProfile();
        }
        catch(Exception $e) {
             return $e->getMessage();
        }
        echo 'Welcome ' . $profile->displayName . '<br>';
        echo 'Your image: <img src="' . $profile->photoURL
             . '">';
        dd($profile);
   });
```

How it works...

After getting our Twitter API credentials, we need to create a configuration file with those credentials and our callback URL.

We then make a Twitter login view, which is a simple link to a route where we do the authentication. The user will then be taken to Twitter to login and/or authorize our site, and then redirected back to our twauth route. Here, we get their display name and their Twitter icon.

At this point, we're just displaying the information that was returned, but we'd also probably want to save the information to our own database.

There's more...

If we're testing this on our local computer using something like MAMP or WAMP, Twitter will NOT allow a callback URL of localhost, but we can use 127.0.0.1 in its place.

Logging in using LinkedIn

If we don't want to worry about storing user's information and credentials, we could use OAuth to authenticate with another service. A popular service to use for logins, especially for business applications, is LinkedIn. With Laravel and the HybridAuth library, we can easily implement OAuth authentication with LinkedIn.

For this recipe, we need to have the HybridAuth package installed and set up as in the *Setting up OAuth with the HybridAuth package* recipe.

To complete this recipe, follow these steps:

1. Create a new app at `https://www.linkedin.com/secure/developer`.

2. Get the API Key and the Secret Key, and in the `app/config` directory, create a file named `li_auth.php`:

```php
<?php
return array(
    "base_url"   => "http://path/to/our/app/liauth/auth",
    "providers"  => array (
        "LinkedIn" => array (
            "enabled" => true,
            "keys"     => array ("key" => "API_KEY",
                "secret" => "SECRET_KEY")
        )
    )
);
```

3. Create a route in `routes.php` for our LinkedIn login button:

```php
Route::get('linkedin', function()
{
    return "<a href='liauth'>Login with LinkedIn</a>";
});
```

4. Make a route to process the LinkedIn information:

```php
Route::get('liauth/{auth?}', function($auth = NULL)
{
    if ($auth == 'auth') {
        try {
            Hybrid_Endpoint::process();
        } catch (Exception $e) {
            return Redirect::to('liauth');
        }
        return;
    }

    try {
```

```
        $oauth = new Hybrid_Auth(app_path()
            . '/config/li_auth.php');
        $provider = $oauth->authenticate('LinkedIn');
        $profile = $provider->getUserProfile();
    }
    catch(Exception $e) {
        return $e->getMessage();
    }
    echo 'Welcome ' . $profile->firstName . ' ' . $profile
        ->lastName . '<br>';
    echo 'Your email: ' . $profile->email . '<br>';
    echo 'Your image: <img src="' . $profile->photoURL
        . '">';
    dd($profile);
});
```

How it works...

After getting our LinkedIn API credentials, we need to create a configuration file with those credentials and our callback URL.

We then make a LinkedIn login view, with a simple link to a route where we do the LinkedIn authentication. The user will then be taken to the LinkedIn site to login and/or authorize our site, and then redirected back to our liauth route. Here, we get their first name, last name, e-mail ID, and their avatar.

At this point, we're just displaying the information that was returned, but we'd also probably want to save the information to our own database.

4

Storing and Using Data

In this chapter, we will cover:

- ▸ Creating data tables using migrations and schemas
- ▸ Querying using raw SQL statements
- ▸ Querying using Fluent
- ▸ Querying using Eloquent ORM
- ▸ Using automatic validation in models
- ▸ Using advanced Eloquent and relationships
- ▸ Creating a CRUD system
- ▸ Importing a CSV using Eloquent
- ▸ Using RSS as a data source
- ▸ Using attributes to change table column names
- ▸ Using a non-Eloquent ORM in Laravel

Introduction

One of the backbones of any web application is the use and manipulation of data. Laravel comes with many handy ways to interact with databases and display their information. In this chapter, we'll begin with some simple database interactions. Then we'll use other, non-databases for our data source, and then work on some customizations for our Laravel application.

Creating data tables using migrations and schemas

Using Laravel, we can easily create our data model using schemas and migrations. In this recipe, we'll see some basic functionality of how Laravel accomplishes this.

Getting ready

For this recipe, we need a standard Laravel installation, as well as a MySQL database configured in our database config file.

How to do it...

To complete this recipe, follow these steps:

1. Install our migrations table from the command prompt, using `artisan`:

```
php artisan migrate:install
```

2. Create a migration to hold our Schema code for creating a new table:

```
php artisan migrate:make create_shows_table
```

3. In our app/database/migrations directory, locate the file that should be named similar to 2012_01_01_222551_create_shows_table.php. Add the schema to create our table and add the columns:

```
class CreateShowsTable extends Migration {

    /**
     * Make changes to the database.
     *
     * @return void
     */
    public function up()
    {
        Schema::create('shows', function($table)
        {
            $table->increments('id');
            $table->string('name', 140);
            $table->integer('rating')->nullable();
            $table->timestamps();
        });
    }

    /**
     * Revert the changes to the database.
     *
```

```
         * @return void
         */
        public function down()
        {
            Schema::drop('shows');
        }
    }
```

4. Run the migration to add the table to the database, using the following command:

   php artisan migrate

5. Create another migration so we can add a column to our table:

   php artisan migrate:make add_actor_to_shows_table

6. In the app/database/migrations directory, find the file that has a name similar to 2012_01_01_222551_add_actor_to_shows_table.php. Add the column to our schema:

```
class AddActorToShowsTable extends Migration {

    /**
     * Make changes to the database.
     *
     * @return void
     */
    public function up()
    {
        Schema::table('shows', function($table)
        {
            $table->string('actor')->nullable();
        });
    }

    /**
     * Revert the changes to the database.
     *
     * @return void
     */
    public function down()
    {
        Schema::table('shows', function($table)
        {
            $table->drop_column('actor');
        });
    }
}
```

7. Run the migration in the command prompt to add the column to our table:

   php artisan migrate

How it works...

Using Laravel's Artisan command-line tool, we run the command to create a migrations table. This will track any migrations and schema changes we make. Then we use Artisan to create a migrations file that will hold the schema for our `shows` table.

In the `shows` schema, we create a simple table to hold a list of TV shows, and how we rate them. The name of the show is set as a string, the rating as an integer, and we use Laravel's default mechanism for creating timestamps. When we run the migration, our table will be created for us.

If we decide we want to add another column in our table, we just create another migration file using Artisan. In this case, we'll be adding a column to hold an actor's name. Our schema will get the table we already created and add the column to it. When we rerun the migration, everything will be updated in the database.

There's more...

We could also have some more boilerplate code created for us by using a couple of command-line switches with Artisan. For example, to create the shows table, we could run this command:

```
php artisan migrate:make create_shows_table -table=show -create
```

Running that command will produce a migration file that includes the following code:

```php
<?php

use Illuminate\Database\Schema\Blueprint;
use Illuminate\Database\Migrations\Migration;

class CreateShowsTable extends Migration {

    /**
     * Run the migrations.
     *
     * @return void
     */
    public function up()
    {
        Schema::create('shows', function(Blueprint $table)
        {
            $table->increments('id');
            $table->timestamps();
        });
    }
```

```
/**
 * Reverse the migrations.
 *
 * @return void
 */
public function down()
{
    Schema::drop('shows');
}

}
```

Querying using raw SQL statements

Laravel provides many ways to access our database. If we have existing queries that we've used before, or if we need something a bit more complicated, we can use raw SQL to access our database.

Getting ready

For this recipe, we'll be using the table created in the *Creating data tables using migrations and schema* recipe.

How to do it...

To complete this recipe, follow these steps:

1. In the command prompt, create a migration so we can add some data:

   php artisan migrate:make add_data_to_shows_table

2. In our app/database/migrations directory, find a file similar to 2012_01_01_222551_add_data_to_shows_table.php, and add some data using raw SQL:

```
class AddDataToShowsTable {

    /**
     * Make changes to the database.
     *
     * @return void
     */

    public function up()
        {
```

```
                    $sql = 'INSERT INTO shows (name, rating, actor)
                        VALUES (?, ?, ?)';
                    $data1 = array('Doctor Who', '9', 'Matt Smith');
                    $data2 = array('Arrested Development', '10', 'Jason
                        Bateman');
                    $data3 = array('Joanie Loves Chachi', '3', 'Scott
                        Baio');
                    DB::insert($sql, $data1);
                    DB::insert($sql, $data2);
                    DB::insert($sql, $data3);
                }


                /**
                 * Revert the changes to the database.
                 *
                 * @return void
                 */
                public function down()
                {
                    $sql = "DELETE FROM shows WHERE name = ?";
                    DB::delete($sql, array('Doctor Who'));
                    DB::delete($sql, array('Arrested Development'));
                    DB::delete($sql, array('Joanie Loves Chachi'));
                }
            }
```

3. Run the migration in the command prompt to add the data:

   php artisan migrate

4. In our `app/models` directory, create a file named `Show.php` and add a method to get the shows:

```
class Show {
    public function allShows($order_by = FALSE,
        $direction = 'ASC')
    {
        $sql = 'SELECT * FROM shows';
        $sql .= $order_by ? ' ORDER BY ' . $order_by
            . ' ' . $direction : '';
        return DB::select($sql);
    }
}
```

5. In our `routes.php` file, create a `Show` route to display the information from the model:

```
Route::get('shows', function()
{
    $shows = new Show();
    $shows_by_rating = $shows->allShows('rating', 'DESC');
    dd($shows_by_rating);
});
```

How it works...

To populate some data in our `shows` table, we first need to create a migration using the Artisan command-line tool. In the migration file's `up` method, we create a simple SQL insert command, and pass in three parameters. We then create three arrays, with the values in the same order as columns in our query. Then we pass the SQL statement variable and array of values to Laravel's `DB::insert()` command. For our `down` method, we use a SQL delete statement, searching by the show's name. Once we run the migration, our data will populate into the table.

Next, we create a model to interact with the database in the frontend. Our model has one method to display all the shows in our table, with optional parameters if we'd like to re-order how they're displayed.

Our route instantiates the Show model and runs the `allShows()` method. To display the results, we use Laravel's `dd()` helper function. At this point, we could pass the data to a view and loop through it to display.

See also

▶   The *Creating data tables using migrations and schema* recipe

Querying using Fluent

Laravel provides many ways to access databases. If we choose not to write raw SQL statements, we can use the Fluent query builder to make things easier.

Getting ready

For this recipe, we'll be using the table created in the *Creating data tables using migrations and schemas* recipe.

How to do it...

To complete this recipe, follow these steps:

1. In the command prompt, create a migration so we can add some data:

   ```
   php artisan migrate:make add_data_to_shows_table
   ```

2. In our app/database/migrations directory, find a file similar to
   2012_01_01_222551_add_data_to_shows_table.php, and add some data
   using the Fluent query builder:

   ```php
   class AddDataToShowsTable {

       /**
        * Make changes to the database.
        *
        * @return void
        */
       public function up()
       {
           $data1 = array('name' => 'Doctor Who',
               'rating' => 9, 'actor' => 'Matt Smith');
           $data2 = array('name' => 'Arrested Development',
               'rating' => 10, 'actor' => 'Jason Bateman');
           $data3 = array('name' => 'Joanie Loves Chachi',
               'rating' => 3, 'actor' => 'Scott Baio');
           DB::table('shows')->insert(array($data1, $data2,
               $data3));
       }

       /**
        * Revert the changes to the database.
        *
        * @return void
        */
       public function down()
       {
           DB::table('shows')
               ->where('name', 'Doctor Who')
               ->orWhere('name', 'Arrested Development')
               ->orWhere('name', 'Joanie Loves Chachi')
               ->delete();
       }
   }
   ```

3. Run the migration to add the data:

```
php artisan migrate
```

4. In our `app/models` directory, create a file named `Show.php` and add a method to get the shows:

```
class Show {
    public function allShows($order_by = FALSE,
        $direction = 'ASC')
    {
        $shows = DB::table('shows');
        return $order_by ? $shows->order_by($order_by,
            $direction)->get() : $shows->get();
    }
}
```

5. In our `routes.php` file, create a `Show` route to display the information from the model:

```
Route::get('shows', function()
{
    $shows = new Show();
    $shows_by_rating = $shows->allShows('rating', 'DESC');
    dd($shows_by_rating);
});
```

How it works...

To populate some data in our `shows` table, we first need to create a migration using the Artisan command-line tool. In the migration file's up method, we create three arrays that hold our values, using the column names as keys. Those arrays are then put into an array and passed to the Fluent `insert` function. The down method uses the `where()` and `orWhere()` functions to locate records by their name, and deletes them. Once we run the migration, our data will populate into the table.

Next, we create a model to interact with the database in the frontend. Our model has one method to display all the shows in our table, with optional parameters if we'd like to reorder how they're displayed.

Our route instantiates the Show model and runs the `allShows()` method. To display the results, we use Laravel's `dd()` helper function. We could also create a view and pass the data there to loop through.

There's more...

Many more fluent methods can be found in Laravel's documentation at `http://laravel.com/docs/queries`.

See also

▶ The *Creating data tables using migrations and schemas* recipe

Querying using Eloquent ORM

Laravel provides many ways to interact with databases. One of the easiest ways is using the Eloquent ORM. It provides a simple and intuitive way to work with data.

Getting ready

For this recipe, we'll be using the table created in the *Creating data tables using migrations and schemas* recipe.

How to do it...

To complete this recipe, follow these steps:

1. In the command prompt, create a migration so we can add some data:

   ```
   php artisan migrate:make add_data_to_shows_table
   ```

2. In our `app/database/migrations` directory, find a file similar to `2012_01_01_222551_add_data_to_shows_table.php`, and add some data using the Fluent query builder:

   ```
   class AddDataToShowsTable {

       /**
        * Make changes to the database.
        *
        * @return void
        */
       public function up()
       {
           $data1 = array('name' => 'Doctor Who',
               'rating' => 9, 'actor' => 'Matt Smith');
           $data2 = array('name' => 'Arrested Development',
               'rating' => 10, 'actor' => 'Jason Bateman');
   ```

```
        $data3 = array('name' => 'Joanie Loves Chachi',
            'rating' => 3, 'actor' => 'Scott Baio');
        DB::table('shows')->insert(array($data1, $data2,
            $data3));
    }


    /**
     * Revert the changes to the database.
     *
     * @return void
     */
    public function down()
    {
        DB::table('shows')
            ->where('name', 'Doctor Who')
            ->orWhere('name', 'Arrested Development')
            ->orWhere('name', 'Joanie Loves Chachi')
            ->delete();
    }
}
```

3. Run the migration to add the data:

   php artisan migrate

4. In our app/models directory, create a file named Show.php that extends
   Eloquent:

```
class Show extends Eloquent{
    public function getTopShows() {
        return $this->where('rating', '>', 5)
            ->orderBy('rating', 'DESC')->get();
    }
}
```

5. In our routes.php file, create a show route to display the information from
   the model:

```
Route::get('shows', function()
{
    $shows = Show::all();
    echo '<h1>All Shows</h1>';
    foreach ($shows as $show)
    {
        echo $show->name . ' - ' . $show->rating . ' - '
            . $show->actor . '<br>';
    }
```

```
$show_object = new Show();
$top_shows = $show_object->getTopShows();
echo '<h1>Top Shows</h1>';
foreach ($top_shows as $top_show)
{
    echo $top_show->name . ' - ' . $top_show->rating
        . ' - ' . $top_show->actor . '<br>';
}

});
```

How it works...

To populate some data in our `shows` table, we first need to create a migration using the Artisan command-line tool. In the migration file's up method, we create three arrays that hold our values, using the column names as keys. Those arrays are then put into an array and passed to the Fluent `insert` function. The `down` method uses the `where()` and `orWhere()` functions to locate records by their name, and deletes them. Once we run the migration, our data will populate into the table.

Next, we create a model to interact with the database in the frontend. For this recipe, all we need to do is extend `Eloquent` and the ORM will automatically take care of everything else. We also add in a method that will return all of the top shows.

Our route calls the `all()` method for our Show ORM object; this will put all the data into the `$shows` variable. Then we do a simple loop through the records and display the fields we want. Next, we get a filtered list by calling the method in the Show model, by only getting records with a rating greater than 5 and ordered by rating.

There's more...

In this recipe, we're displaying all the data inside the route. Ideally, we'd pass the data into a view and display it there.

See also

▶ The *Creating data tables using migrations and schemas* recipe

Using automatic validation in models

When validating data that's being sent to the database, ideally we should put the rules and validation in our model. In this recipe we'll see one way to accomplish this.

Getting ready

For this recipe, we need a standard Laravel installation with a configured MySQL database. We also need our migrations table set up by running the Artisan command `php artisan migrate:install`.

How to do it...

To complete this recipe, follow these steps:

1. In the command prompt, create a migration for a simple `users` table:

```
php artisan migrate:make create_users_table
```

2. Create the schema in the migration file. The file is located in the `app/database/migrations` directory and will be named something like `2012_01_01_222551_create_users_table.php`:

```php
use Illuminate\Database\Migrations\Migration;

class CreateUsersTable extends Migration {

    /**
     * Make changes to the database.
     *
     * @return void
     */
    public function up()
    {
        Schema::create('users', function($table)
        {
            $table->increments('id');
            $table->string('username', 100);
            $table->string('email', 100);
            $table->timestamps();
        });
    }

    /**
     * Revert the changes to the database.
     *
     * @return void
     */
    public function down()
    {
        Schema::drop('users');
    }
}
```

3. Run the migration:

```
php artisan migrate
```

4. Create a file named `User.php` in our `app/models` directory. If there's already a file named `User.php`, we can just rename it:

```php
<?php
class User extends Eloquent {

    protected $table = 'users';

    private $rules = array(
        'email' => 'required|email',
        'username' => 'required|min:6'
    );

    public function validate($input) {
        return Validator::make($input, $this->rules);
    }
}
```

5. Make a route that loads the ORM and tries to save some data:

```php
$user = new User();
    $input = array();

    $input['email'] = 'racerx@example.com';
    $input['username'] = 'Short';
    $valid = $user->validate($input);
    if ($valid->passes()) {
        echo 'Everything is Valid!';
        // Save to the database
    } else {
        var_dump($valid->messages());
    }
```

How it works...

To begin, we create a migration for a basic `users` table. In our schema, we set up a table with an ID, username, e-mail ID, and timestamps. Then run the migration to create the table in the database.

Next, we set up our User model and extend `Eloquent`. We need to create our rules, using a private variable named as `$rules` that contains an array of the validation rules we want to check. In our model, we create a `validate` method. This will run our input through Laravel's `Validator` using the rules we have just set up.

In our route, we create a new user and add some values. Before we save, we run the input through the `validate` method; if it fails, we can loop through the validation error messages. If it passes, we could then save the input to our database

There's more...

There are a few other ways to validate our data using models. One way is to use a package that will handle most of the validation work for us. One great package to use is Ardent, which can be found at `https://github.com/laravelbook/ardent`.

Using advanced Eloquent and relationships

One of the great things about using Laravel's Eloquent ORM is the ease with which we can interact with multiple tables that have foreign keys and pivot tables. In this recipe, we'll see how easy it is to set up our models and run queries against joined tables.

Getting ready

For this recipe, we'll be using the `shows` and `users` tables created in the previous recipes *Creating data tables using migrations and schemas* and *Using automatic validation in models*.

How to do it...

To complete this recipe, follow these steps:

1. In the command prompt, create a migration for a new pivot table:

   ```
   php artisan migrate:make create_show_user
   ```

2. Open the migrations file in the `app/database/migrations` directory and add the schema:

   ```
   use Illuminate\Database\Migrations\Migration;

   class CreateShowUser extends Migration {

       /**
        * Make changes to the database.
        *
        * @return void
        */
       public function up()
       {
   ```

```
        Schema::create('show_user', function($table)
        {
            $table->increments('id');
            $table->integer('user_id');
            $table->integer('show_id');
            $table->timestamps();
        });
    }


    /**
     * Revert the changes to the database.
     *
     * @return void
     */
    public function down()
    {
        Schema::drop('show_user');
    }
}
```

3. Run the migration:

    php artisan migrate

4. Create a `User.php` file in the `app/model` directory:

    ```
    class User extends Eloquent {
        public function shows()
        {
            return $this->belongsToMany ('Show');
        }
    }
    ```

5. Create a `Show.php` file in our `app/model` directory:

    ```
    class Show extends Eloquent {
        public function users()
        {
            return $this->belongsToMany ('User');
        }
    }
    ```

6. Make a route in `routes.php` to add a new user and attach two shows:

    ```
    Route::get('add-show', function()
    {
        // Create a new User
        $user = new User();
    ```

```
$user->username = 'John Doe';
$user->email = 'johndoe@example.com';
$user->save();

// Attach two Shows
$user->shows()->attach(1);
$user->shows()->attach(3);

foreach($user->shows()->get() as $show) {
    var_dump($show->name);
}
});
```

7. Make a route to get all the users attached to a show:

```
Route::get('view-show', function()
{
    $show = Show::find(1)->users;
    dd($show);
});
```

How it works...

Our first task is to create a pivot table that will join our `users` tables with our `shows` table. In our migration's schema, we need to add columns for our `user_id` and a `show_id`. We then run the migration to get the table set up in our database.

To set up our models, we need to create a function that will return our many-to-many relationship. In our User model, we create the `shows()` function that points to our Show model for the relationship. In the Show model, we create a function named `users()` that points to our User model. With this set up, we can now run queries against both tables with ease.

Next, we create a route that will add in a new user. Once we save the user, we create the relationship with the shows by using the `attach()` method, and pass in the ID of the show we want to attach. After this, if we were to look in our `show_user` table, we'd see two records—one with our new user's ID and the show ID 1, and another with the show ID of 3. By running the `get()` method in our route, we can loop through the records and see which show names are joined to our user.

Our next route will take a show and get all the users that are joined. In our case, we get the show with the ID of 1, and then get all of the users. Using Laravel's `dd()` helper, we can see our results.

There's more...

Database relationships can get fairly complicated and this recipe merely scratches the surface of what can be done. To learn more about how Laravel's Eloquent ORM uses relationships, view the documentation at `http://laravel.com/docs/eloquent#many-to-many`.

Creating a CRUD system

To interact with our database, we might need to create a CRUD (create, read, update, and delete) system. That way, we add and alter our data without needing a separate database client. This recipe will be using a RESTful controller for our CRUD system.

Getting ready

For this recipe, we'll be building on the User tables created in the recipe *Using automatic validation in models*.

How to do it...

To complete this recipe, follow these steps:

1. In the `app/controllers` directory, create a file named as `UsersController.php` and add the following code:

```php
<?php

class UsersController extends BaseController {

    public function getIndex()
    {
        $users = User::all();
        return View::make('users.index')->with('users',
            $users);
    }

    public function getCreate()
    {
        return View::make('users.create');
    }
```

```php
public function postCreate()
{
    $user = new User();
    $user->username = Input::get('username');
    $user->email = Input::get('email');
    $user->save();
    return Redirect::to('users');
}

public function getRecord($id)
{
    $user = User::find($id);
    return View::make('users.record')->with('user',
        $user);
}

public function putRecord()
{
    $user = User::find(Input::get('user_id'));
    $user->username = Input::get('username');
    $user->email = Input::get('email');
    $user->save();
    return Redirect::to('users');
}

public function deleteRecord()
{
    $user = User::find(Input::get('user_id'))
        ->delete();
    return Redirect::to('users');
}
}
```

2. In our `routes.php` file, add a route to the controller:

   Route::controller('users', 'UsersController');

3. In the `app/views` directory, create another directory named as `users`, create a file named `index.php` in that, and add the following code:

```html
<style>
table, th, td {
    border:1px solid #444
}
</style>
<table>
    <thead>
        <tr>
            <th>User ID</th>
```

```
                <th>User Name</th>
                <th>Email</th>
                <th>Actions</th>
            </tr>
        </thead>
        <tbody>
            <?php foreach($users as $user): ?>
                <tr>
                    <td><?php echo $user->id ?></td>
                    <td><?php echo $user->username ?></td>
                    <td><?php echo $user->email ?></td>
                    <td>
                        <a href="users/record/<?php echo $user
                            ->id ?>">Edit</a>
                        <form action="users/record"
                            method="post">
                            <input type="hidden" name="_method"
                                value="DELETE">
                            <input type="hidden" name="user_id"
                                value="<?php echo $user->id
                                ?>">
                            <input type="submit"
                                value="Delete">
                        </form>
                    </td>
                </tr>
            <?php endforeach; ?>
        </tbody>
    </table>
    <a href="users/create">Add New User</a>
```

4. In the `app/views/users` directory, create a new file named `create.php` and the form as follows:

```
<form action="create" method="post">
    Username:<br>
    <input name="username"><br>
    Email<br>
    <input name="email"><br>
    <input type="submit">
</form>
```

5. In the `app/views/users` directory, add a file named `record.php` and use the following form:

```
<form action="" method="post">
    <input type="hidden" name="_method" value="put">
    <input type="hidden" name="user_id" value="<?php echo
        $user->id ?>">
```

```
    Username:<br>
    <input name="username" value="<?php echo $user
        ->username ?>"><br>
    Email<br>
    <input name="email" value="<?php echo $user->email
        ?>"><br>
    <input type="submit">
</form>
```

How it works...

In our controller, our method names can be prepended with the HTTP verb we want to use. We then add in the route in our routes file, so it points to the correct place.

Our first method will generate a list of all our users. We pass the users to our view, and then loop through them and display them in a simple table.

Under that table, we have a link to our second method to add a new user. Our `getRreate()` method displays a simple form, and that form gets posted and saved. After saving, we're redirected back to the list page.

To edit a record, we create a `getRecord()` method that gets the record's ID passed to it. Our view is a form that is automatically filled in with the values of the user for the ID that was passed in. Since we're doing an update, we want to use the `put` verb; to accomplish this, we need a hidden field with the name `_method` and the value of the request we want to use. When the form is submitted, Laravel will send it to the `putRecord()` method, and update the information.

Finally, to delete a record, we create a simple form that has the hidden field named `_method` and the value `DELETE`. When submitted, Laravel will send it to the `deleteRecord()` method, and the user will be removed from the database.

There's more...

Please be aware that this is the most basic of CRUD systems. For a full system, we'd need to add validation and error checking any time we add or edit our data.

Importing a CSV using Eloquent

When working with data, there are many different sources and file types that we may encounter. A common type is a CSV, or comma separated value, file. In this recipe, we'll take a CSV file's contents and insert them into our database.

Getting ready

To get started, we need to have a standard Laravel installation that's configured with a MySQL database. We also need to have our migrations table created by running the Artisan command, `php artisan migrate:install`.

How to do it...

To complete this recipe, follow these steps:

1. In a text editor, create a file named `scifi.csv`, save it to your application's `public` folder. Add in the following data:

   ```
   Spock,Star Trek
   Kirk,Star Trek
   Luke,Star Wars
   Lando,Star Wars
   Deckard,Blade Runner
   Dave,2001
   ```

2. In the command prompt, create a migration:

   ```
   php artisan migrate:make create_scifi_table
   ```

3. Open the migration file that was just created and add in our schema:

   ```php
   use Illuminate\Database\Migrations\Migration;

   class CreateScifiTable extends Migration {

       /**
        * Make changes to the database.
        *
        * @return void
        */
       public function up()
       {
           Schema::create('scifi', function($table)
           {
               $table->increments('id');
               $table->string('character');
               $table->string('movie');
               $table->timestamps();
           });
       }
   ```

```
/**
 * Revert the changes to the database.
 *
 * @return void
 */
public function down()
{
    Schema::drop('scifi');
}
}
```

4. Run the migration to create the table:

   php artisan migrate

5. Create a model in the app/models directory named as Scifi.php:

   ```
   class Scifi extends Eloquent {
       protected $table = 'scifi';
   }
   ```

6. Create a new route to process our CSV and save the results:

   ```
   Route::get('csv', function()
   {
       if (($handle = fopen(public_path() .. '/scifi.csv',
           'r')) !== FALSE)
       {
           while (($data = fgetcsv($handle, 1000, ',')) !==
               FALSE)
           {
               $scifi = new Scifi();
               $scifi->character = $data[0];
               $scifi->movie = $data[1];
               $scifi->save();
           }
           fclose($handle);
       }

       return Scifi::all();
   });
   ```

How it works...

Our first step is to create a simple CSV file, with the names of some science fiction characters and the movies in which they appeared. Then we create a migration and a schema that will add a scifi table with fields we want to save.

For our model, we extend `Eloquent` and add in a protected variable named `$table` that is set to our table's name. Since we're not pluralizing `scifi` for our table's name, we need to let Eloquent know which table to use.

In our route, we open the file and loop through the data using PHP's built-in functions `fopen()` and `fgetcsv()` respectively. In each loop, we create a new `Scifi` object, then set the values to the data we get from the CSV file. After looping, we close the file.

To see our data, we call the `all()` method on our `Scifi` object and return it to display all the data.

Using RSS as a data source

Many blogs and news sites offer RSS feeds of their content. Using Laravel, we can get those feeds and display them as a feed reader, or even save them in our own database.

Getting ready

For this recipe, we just need a standard Laravel installation, and RSS URL to use.

How to do it...

To complete this recipe, follow this step:

1. Create a new route in our `routes.php` file to read in the RSS:

```
Route::get('rss', function()
{
    $source = 'http://rss.cnn.com/rss/cnn_topstories.rss';

    $headers = get_headers($source);
    $response = substr($headers[0], 9, 3);
    if ($response == '404')
    {
        return 'Invalid Source';
    }

    $data = simplexml_load_string
        (file_get_contents($source));

    if (count($data) == 0)
    {
        return 'No Posts';
    }
```

```
$posts = '';
foreach($data->channel->item as $item)
{
    $posts .= '<h1><a href="' . $item->link . '">'
        . $item->title . '</a></h1>';
    $posts .= '<h4>' . $item->pubDate . '</h4>';
    $posts .= '<p>' . $item->description . '</p>';
    $posts .= '<hr><hr>';
}
return $posts;
});
```

How it works...

We create a route to hold our RSS reader. Then we set our $source variable to whichever RSS feed we want to consume.

To make sure our source is still active, we use the PHP function get_headers(), and grab the response code. If the code is 404, then the URL doesn't work.

Next, we get the contents from the URL, and use the simplexml_load_string() function to process the XML in the feed. If that feed actually has data, we can loop through it and display the information. We could also save it to our database as we loop.

Using attributes to change table column names

Sometimes we may be working with a database that was created using less-than-logical column names. In those cases, we can use Laravel's Eloquent ORM to allows us to interact with the table using more standardized names, without having to make database changes.

Getting ready

For this recipe, we need a standard Laravel installation, a properly configured MySQL database, and our migrations table set up by running the command php artisan migrate:install.

How to do it...

To complete this recipe, follow these steps:

1. Create a migration for our table with the column name odd, in the command prompt:

   ```
   php artisan migrate:make create_odd_table --table=odd --create
   ```

2. Create a migration to add some data to the table, in the command prompt:

```
php artisan migrate:make add_data_to_odd_table
```

3. In the app/database/migrations folder, open the create_odd_table migration and add the schema:

```php
use Illuminate\Database\Schema\Blueprint;
use Illuminate\Database\Migrations\Migration;

class CreateOddTable extends Migration {

    /**
     * Run the migrations.
     *
     * @return void
     */
    public function up()
    {
        Schema::create('odd', function(Blueprint $table)
        {
            $table->increments('MyIDcolumn');
            $table->string('MyUsernameGoesHere');
            $table->string('ThisIsAnEmail');
            $table->timestamps();
        });
    }

    /**
     * Reverse the migrations.
     *
     * @return void
     */
    public function down()
    {
        Schema::drop('odd');
    }
}
```

4. In the app/database/migrations directory, open the add_data_to_odd_table file and add some data:

```php
use Illuminate\Database\Migrations\Migration;

class AddDataToOddTable extends Migration {

    /**
```

```
     * Make changes to the database.
     *
     * @return void
     */
    public function up()
    {
        $data1 = array('MyUsernameGoesHere' => 'John Doe',
            'ThisIsAnEmail' => 'johndoe@example.com');
        $data2 = array('MyUsernameGoesHere' => 'Jane Doe',
            'ThisIsAnEmail' => 'janedoe@example.com');
        DB::table('odd')->insert(array($data1, $data2));
    }


    /**
     * Revert the changes to the database.
     *
     * @return void
     */
    public function down()
    {
        DB::table('odd')->delete();
    }
}
```

5. In the command prompt, run the migration:

    php artisan migrate

6. In the `app/models` directory, create a new file named as `Odd.php` and create the getters:

```
class Odd extends Eloquent {
    protected $table = 'odd';

    public function getIdAttribute($value) {
        return $this->attributes['MyIDcolumn'];
    }

    public function getUsernameAttribute($value) {
        return $this->attributes['MyUsernameGoesHere'];
    }

    public function getEmailAttribute($value) {
        return $this->attributes['ThisIsAnEmail'];
    }
}
```

7. Make a new route in `routes.php` to access the table using the regular column name:

```
Route::get('odd', function()
{
    $odds = Odd::all();
    foreach($odds as $odd)
    {
        echo $odd->MyIDcolumn . ' - ' . $odd
            ->MyUsernameGoesHere . ' - ' . $odd
            ->ThisIsAnEmail . '<br>';
    }
});
```

8. Make another route, using the more standard column names:

```
Route::get('notodd', function()
{
    $odds = Odd::all();
    foreach($odds as $odd)
    {
        echo $odd->id . ' - ' . $odd->username . ' - '
            . $odd->email . '<br>';
    }
});
```

How it works...

To begin, we create two migration files. One file will actually create the tables with the non-standard column name, and the other will populate the data.

For our model, we extend `Eloquent` and add a few `get` methods. Inside each `get` method, set our attributes, which tells Eloquent which column name we want to use. Now, since we have the `getUsernameAttribute()` method in our model, whenever we try access the username in our object, it will actually access the column name we defined.

Then, we create a route that will pull all of the records from our `odd` table, and loop through. For our first route, we access the column using their real names. In our second route, we use the new names. If we access both of these routes, we would see the exact same information.

Using a non-Eloquent ORM in Laravel

Laravel's Eloquent ORM is easy-to-use and very efficient. However, there are many different PHP ORMs and we may decide we prefer another ORM. In this recipe, we'll install the RedBean ORM and use it for our data.

Getting ready

For this recipe, we'll be using the RedBean ORM. You'll need to download it from `http://www.redbeanphp.com/manual/installing`, and unzip the file. Then move the file `rb.php` to the `app/libraries` directory of your app.

How to do it...

To complete this recipe, follow these steps:

1. In the `composer.json` file, make our autoloader load our `libraries` directory. The `autoload` section should look similar to this:

    ```
    "autoload": {
        "classmap": [
            "app/commands",
            "app/controllers",
            "app/models",
            "app/database/migrations",
            "app/database/seeds",
            "app/tests/TestCase.php",
            "app/libraries"
        ],
    }
    ```

2. In the command prompt, dump our autoloader:

    ```
    php composer.phar dump-autoload
    ```

3. In our `routes.php` file, we'll add a simple configuration:

    ```
    $db_setup = Config::get('database.connections.mysql');
    R::setup('mysql:host=' . $db_setup['host'] . ';dbname='
        . $db_setup['database'], $db_setup['username'],
        $db_setup['password']);
    ```

4. Create a route that will add some data and then display it:

    ```
    Route::get('orm', function()
    {
        $superhero = R::dispense('superheroes');
        $superhero->name = 'Spiderman';
        $superhero->city = 'New York';
        $superhero->age = 24;

        $id1 = R::store($superhero);
    ```

```
$superhero = R::dispense('superheroes');
$superhero->name = 'Superman';
$superhero->city = 'Metropolis';
$superhero->age = 50;

$id2 = R::store($superhero);

$superhero = R::dispense('superheroes');
$superhero->name = 'Batman';
$superhero->city = 'Gotham';
$superhero->age = 36;

$id3 = R::store($superhero);

$heroes = R::batch('superheroes',array($id1, $id2,
    $id3));

foreach ($heroes as $hero)
{
    echo $hero->name . ' - ' . $hero->city . ' - '
        . $hero->age . '<br>';
}
});
```

How it works...

After adding the RedBean file to our `libraries` directory, we need to update our composer file's autoloader so that it will load the `rb.php` file.

Setting up the database configuration can be done in various places but, for this recipe, we'll set it up at the top of our routes file. So we can keep our database information in one place, we use Laravel's database configuration to get it set up.

Once all that is done, we're ready to use RedBean in our application. In our route, we're creating three superheroes and adding them to the `superheroes` table. With RedBean, if the table doesn't exist, it will automatically create it for you and add in the relevant columns.

Finally, we get three records and can loop through them to display the information.

There's more...

RedBeans has many features that might be useful as a replacement ORM. To see all the features, visit its official manual at `http://redbeanphp.com/manual/`.

5

Using Controllers and Routes for URLs and APIs

In this chapter, we will cover:

- ► Creating a basic controller
- ► Creating a route using a closure
- ► Creating a RESTful controller
- ► Using advanced routing
- ► Using a filter on the route
- ► Using route groups
- ► Building a RESTful API with routes
- ► Using named routes
- ► Using a subdomain in your route

Introduction

In this chapter, we'll go through some ways to use Laravel's routing system. There are two basic ways to route our application: either setting the routes in the `routes.php` file with closures or using controllers. We'll see the power that each of these methods holds and show how they can be used in our application.

Creating a basic controller

Model-View-Controller (**MVC**) patterns are very popular in PHP frameworks. In this recipe, we'll create a simple controller that extends another base controller.

Getting ready

To start, we just need a standard Laravel installation.

How to do it...

To complete this recipe, follow these steps:

1. In the `app/controllers` directory, create a file named `UsersController.php` and type the following code in to it:

```php
<?php
class UsersController extends BaseController {

    public function actionIndex()
    {
        return "This is a User Index page";
    }

    public function actionAbout()
    {
        return "This is a User About page";
    }
}
```

2. Then, in the `routes.php` file, add the following lines:

```php
Route::get('users', 'UsersController@actionIndex');
Route::get('users/about', 'UsersController@actionAbout');
```

3. Test the controller by going to `http://your-server/users` and `http://your-server/users/about`, where `your-server` is the URL to your app.

How it works...

In our User controller (and pretty much in any other controller that we create), we start by extending the base controller. If we look in the `BaseController.php` file, we see only one method, the `setupLayout()` method, which is used for our layout views. The base controller could also be used if there's some code that we want to run on every page of the site.

Back in the User controller, we define two methods for our Index and About page, with each method prefixed by `action`. For our purposes, we're just returning a single string, but this would be where all of our controller logic would go and where we would set the view to be displayed.

So that Laravel is able to parse the URL and determine which controller and methods to use, we need to register the routes in our `routes` file. Now, in our browser, when we go to `/users` (or `/users/index`), we'll be taken to our Index page, while `/users/about` will take us to our About page.

Creating a route using a closure

If we decide not to use an MVC pattern, we can create our routes by using a closure, or anonymous function.

Getting ready

For this recipe, we just need a standard Laravel installation.

How to do it...

To complete this recipe, follow these steps:

1. In the `app/routes.php` file, add a route as follows:

```
Route::get('hello/world', function()
{
  $hello = 'Hello ';
  $world = 'World!';
  return $hello . $world;
});
```

2. Open your browser and test the route by visiting `http://your-server/hello/world`, where `your-server` is the URL to your app.

How it works...

Routes in Laravel are considered RESTful, which means they respond to various different HTTP verbs. Most of the time, when simply viewing web pages, we use the `GET` verb, as in `Route::get`. Our first parameter is the URL that we're using for the route, and it can be pretty much any valid URL string. In our case, when a user goes to `hello/world`, it will use this route. After that is our closure, or anonymous function.

In the closure, we can pull in any data from our model, do whatever logic we want, and call the views we want to use. In our example case, we're just setting a couple of variables and returning their concatenated value.

Creating a RESTful controller

There may be a time when we want to have a RESTful web application, such as when building an API. To accomplish this, we need our routes to respond to various HTTP requests. The routes with closures are already set up this way, but in this recipe, we'll stay in the MVC pattern and create a controller that is RESTful.

Getting ready

For this recipe, we need a standard Laravel installation and the code from the *Creating a basic controller* recipe.

How to do it...

To complete this recipe, follow these steps:

1. In the User controller, replace the code with the following code:

```php
<?php
class  UsersController extends BaseController {

  public function getIndex()
  {
    $my_form = "<form method='post'>
                        <input name='text' value='Testing'>
                        <input type='submit'>
                        </form>";
    return $my_form;

  }
  public function postIndex()
  {
    dd(Input::all());
  }

  public function getAbout()
  {
      return "This is a User About page";
  }
}
```

2. In `routes.php`, add the route to our controller:

```php
Route::controller('users', 'UsersController');
```

3. In your browser, go to http://your-server/users (where your-server is the URL of your web server) and click on the **Submit** button.

4. In the browser, go to http://your-server/users/about.

How it works...

The two main differences between a RESTful and non-RESTful controller are renaming the methods to have the HTTP request they respond to as a prefix and registering our routes with `Route::controller()`.

Our `getIndex()` method is the default method when we go to `/users`, since most page views are `GET` requests. In this example, we're returning a very simple form that will post the input back to itself. However, since the form is using a `POST` request, it will trigger the `postIndex()` method, and that's where the form can be processed. In our example, we're just using the `dd()` helper of Laravel to display the submitted form input.

Using advanced routing

When creating routes that require parameters, we may need to use more advanced features. Using Laravel and regular expressions, we can make sure that our routes only respond to certain URLs.

Getting ready

For this recipe, we need a standard Laravel installation.

How to do it...

To complete this recipe, follow these steps:

1. In our `routes.php` file, add the following code:

```
Route::get('tvshow/{show?}/{year?}', function($show = null, $year
= null)
{
  if (!$show && !$year)
  {
    return 'You did not pick a show.';
  }
  elseif (!$year)
  {
      return 'You picked the show <strong>' . $show . '</strong>';
  }

  return 'You picked the show <strong>' . $show .
    '</strong> from the year <em>' . $year . '</em>.';
})
->where('year', '\d{4}');
```

2. Open a browser and test the route by typing something such as `http://your-server/tvshow/MASH/1981` (where `your-server` is the URL for your server) in the address bar.

How it works...

We start by having our route respond to a GET request for `tvshow`. If we want to pass parameters to the route, we need to set up wildcards. We can use as many parameters as we'd like and name them whatever we'd like as long as we pass the same name to the function. For this recipe, we want to get a show title, and to make this parameter optional, we add the question mark at the end.

For our second parameter, we want a `year`. In this case, it has to be a four digit number. To use a regular expression, we chain the `where()` method to our route with the name of the parameter and the expression. In this example, we want only numbers, (\d), and there have to be four of them, ({4}). The question mark in the route's parameter makes the field optional.

In our closure, we set variables for each wildcard using the same name we set. To make them optional, we set each variable default to `null`. Then we check to see if the parameters were set, and if so, return an appropriate message.

Using a filter on the route

A powerful feature of Laravel is adding filters that can run both before and after a request is made to our application. In this recipe, we'll explore these filters.

Getting ready

For this recipe, we just need a standard Laravel installation.

How to do it...

To complete this recipe, follow these steps:

1. In our `routes.php` file, add a route only accessible to admins with filters attached:

```
Route::get('admin-only', array('before' => 'checkAdmin', 'after'
=> 'logAdmin', function()
{
  return 'Hello there, admin!';
}));
```

2. Add in the two filters in our `filters.php` file:

```
Route::filter('checkAdmin', function()
{
  if ('admin' !== Session::get('user_type'))
  {
    return 'You are not an Admin. Go Away!';
  }
});


Route::filter('logAdmin', function()
{
  Log::info('Admin logged in on ' . date('m/d/Y'));
});
```

3. Create a route where we can set the admin session:

```
Route::get('set-admin', function()
{
  Session::put('user_type', 'admin');
  return Redirect::to('admin-only');
});
```

4. Test the route by going to `http://your-server/admin-only` (where `your-server` is the URL for your server) and notice the results. Then, go to `set-admin` and see those results.

5. Go to the `app/storage/logs` directory and view the logfiles.

How it works...

In our `admin-only` route, instead of just adding the closure, we add an array with the closure as the last parameter. For our purposes, we want to check that the `user_type` session is set to `admin` before accessing the route. We also want to log each time someone accesses the route, but only after the page is processed.

In our `before` filter, we do a simple check of a session, and if that session doesn't equal `admin`, we return a notice and stop the route from returning its message. If the session does equal `admin`, the route proceeds as normal.

After the route is accessed, we create a log of the visit along with the date the route was accessed.

At this point, if we went to `admin-only` in our browser, the `before` filter would kick in and display the error message. Then, if we went to our logs directory and looked at the log, it would show the time of the attempt, the name of the log message, and the response. For us, it would show **You are not an Admin. Go Away!**.

To make the route accessible, we create another route that simply sets the session we want and redirect back to our `admin-only` page. If we visit `set-admin`, it should automatically direct us to `admin-only` and display the success page. Also, if we look in our logs, we'll see the line for our successful attempt.

There's more...

This is a very rudimentary authentication method simply to show the usefulness of filters. For better authentication, use Laravel's built-in methods.

Using route groups

When creating a web app, we may find a few routes that need the same URL prefix or filter. Using Laravel's route groups, we can easily apply these to multiple routes.

Getting ready

For this recipe, we just need a standard installation of Laravel.

How to do it...

To complete this recipe, follow these steps:

1. In our `app/filters.php` file, create a filter to check for a user:

```
Route::filter('checkUser', function()
{
    if ('user' !== Session::get('profile'))
    {
        return 'You are not Logged In. Go Away!';
    }
});
```

2. In the `app/routes.php` file, create a route that can set our profile session:

```
Route::get('set-profile', function()
{
    Session::set('profile', 'user');
    return Redirect::to('profile/user');
});
```

3. In `routes.php`, create our route group:

```
Route::group(array('before' => 'checkUser', 'prefix' =>
'profile'), function()
{
    Route::get('user', function()
    {
        return 'I am logged in! This is my user
                profile.';
    });
    Route::get('friends', function()
    {
      return 'This would be a list of my friends';
    });
});
```

4. In our browser, we then go to `http://path/to/our/server/profile/user`, where we will get an error. If we then go to `http://path/to/our/server/set-profile`, it will redirect us and show the correct page.

How it works...

The first thing we need to do is create a filter. This simple filter will check a session name, `profile`, to see if it equals `user`. If not, it won't let us proceed any further.

Back in our routes, we then create a route that will set the `profile` session for us and then redirect us to the route group. Setting the session would normally be done after logging in, but here we're just testing to make sure it works.

Finally, we create our route group. For this group, we want every route within it to run through the `checkUser` filter before allowing access. We also want these routes to have `profile/` come before them. We do this by adding them to the array just before we call the group's closure. Now, any route we create inside this group must pass the filter and will be accessible using the `profile` prefix.

Building a RESTful API with routes

A common need for a modern web application is having an API that third-parties can run queries against. Since Laravel is built with RESTful patterns as a focus, it's quite easy to build a full API with very little work.

Getting ready

For this recipe, we need a standard Laravel installation with a properly configured MySQL database tied into our application.

How to do it...

To complete this recipe, follow these steps:

1. Open the command line, go to the root directory of the Laravel installation, and create a migration for our table using the following:

```
php artisan migrate:make create_shows_table
```

2. In the app/database/migrations directory, find the file similar to 2012_12_01_222821_create_shows_table.php and create the schema for our table as follows:

```php
<?php

use Illuminate\Database\Migrations\Migration;

class CreateShowsTable extends Migration {

    /**
     * Run the migrations.
     *
     * @return void
     */
    public function up()
    {
      Schema::create('shows', function($table)
      {
          $table->increments('id');
          $table->string('name');
          $table->integer('year');
          $table->timestamps();
      });

    }

    /**
     * Reverse the migrations.
     *
     * @return void
     */
    public function down()
    {
      Schema::drop('shows');
    }
}
```

3. Back in the command line, run the migration as follows:

```
php artisan migrate
```

4. Create another migration to add some test data:

```
php artisan migrate:make add_shows_data
```

5. In the app/database/migrations folder, open the add_shows_data file and add the query as follows:

```php
<?php

use Illuminate\Database\Migrations\Migration;

class AddShowsData extends Migration {

    /**
     * Run the migrations.
     *
     * @return void
     */
    public function up()
    {
        $shows = array(
                array(
                        'name' => 'Happy Days',
                        'year' => 1981
                ),
                array(
                        'name' => 'Seinfeld',
                        'year' => 1998
                ),
                array(
                        'name' => 'Arrested Development',
                        'year' => 2006
                )
        );
        DB::table('shows')->insert($shows);
    }

    /**
     * Reverse the migrations.
     *
     * @return void
     */
    public function down()
    {
      DB::table('shows')->delete();
    }
}
```

6. In the command line, run the migration as follows:

```
php artisan migrate
```

7. In the app/models directory, create a file named Show.php and add the following code to it:

```php
<?php
class Show extends Eloquent {
    protected $table = 'shows';
}
```

8. In routes.php, create a route to return a JSON of all the shows or a single show as follows:

```php
Route::get('show/{id?}', function($id = null)
{
    if (!$id)
    {
        return Show::all();
    }
    if ($show = Show::find($id))
    {
        return $show;
    }
});
```

9. Create a route that will add in new shows as follows:

```php
Route::post('show', function()
{
    $show = new Show;
    $show->name = Input::get('name');
    $show->year = Input::get('year');
    $show->save();
    return $show;
});
```

10. Create a route that will delete a record:

```php
Route::delete('show/{id}', function($id)
{
    if ($show = Show::find($id))
    {
        $show->delete();
        return json_encode(array('message' => 'Record ' . $id
        . ' deleted.'));
    }
});
```

11. Create a route to update a record:

```
Route::put('show/{id}', function($id)
{
  if ($show = Show::find($id))
  {
      if (Input::get('name')) {
          $show->name = Input::get('name');
    }
      if (Input::get('year')) {
          $show->year = Input::get('year');
      }

      $show->save();
      return $show;
  }
});
```

12. Make a route to hold our add and edit `show form`:

```
Route::get('show-form/{id}', function($id = null)
{
  $data = array();

  if ($id)
  {
      if (!$show = Show::find($id))
      {
        return 'No show with that ID';
      }

      $data = array(
          'id'     => $id,
          'method' => 'PUT',
          'name'   => $show->name,
          'year'   => $show->year
      );
  }
  else
  {
      $data = array(
          'id'     => '',
          'method' => 'POST',
          'name'   => '',
          'year'   => ''
      );
  }
  return View::make('show-form', $data);
});
```

13. Make a route to show a list so we can delete a show:

```
Route::get('show-delete', function()
{
  $shows = Show::all();
  return View::make('show-delete')->with('shows',
   $shows);
});
```

14. In our `app/views` folder, create a file named `show-form.php` and add the following code to it:

```
<?php echo Form::open(array('url' => 'show/' . $id, 'method' =>
$method)) ?>
<?php echo Form::label('name', 'Show Name: ') . Form::text('name',
$name) ?>
<br>
<?php echo Form::label('year', 'Show Year: ') . Form::text('year',
$year) ?>
<br>
<?php echo Form::submit() ?>
<?php echo Form::close() ?>
```

15. Then, in `app/views`, create a file named `show-delete.php` and add the following code to it:

```
<?php foreach ($shows as $show): ?>
  <?php echo Form::open(array('url' => 'show/' .
  $show->id, 'method' => 'DELETE')) ?>
  <?php echo Form::label('name', 'Show Name: ') .
  $show->name ?>
  <?php echo Form::submit('Delete') ?>
  <?php echo Form::close() ?>
<?php endforeach; ?>
```

16. Test it out by going to the `show-form` and `show-delete` routes in the browser.

How it works...

Our first step is to create our tables with the data we want to use. Using artisan and migrations, we create a shows table and then add in some test data.

For our routes, we're going to respond to four different HTTP verbs, GET, POST, PUT, and DELETE, but all at the same URL, show. The GET request will serve two purposes. First, if no ID is passed in the URL, it will display the entire list from the database. Second, if there is an ID, it will display the single record. By returning the eloquent object directly, it will automatically take our object and display it as JSON.

Our next route responds to the `POST` request and will add a new record in the database. It will then display the record that was saved as JSON.

Then, we add a route that responds to the `DELETE` request. It takes the `id` parameter, deletes the record, and displays JSON that the deletion was successful.

Lastly, we have a route responding to a `PUT` request with an `id` parameter. This route will load in the record for the passed in ID and then edit the values. If it updates correctly, it displays a JSON of the updated record.

To show the API in action, we need to create a form to add and update the records. Our `show-form` route checks to see if an ID was passed in, and if so, it creates a form using the `PUT` method and loads the record's values into the fields. If no ID is set, we create a blank form using the `POST` method.

If we want to delete a record, our `show-delete` route will display a list of shows and a delete button next to each one. Those buttons are actually part of a form that uses the `DELETE` method.

We could also test the routes using `curl` in the command line. For example, to get the full list, use the following line of code:

```
curl -X GET http://path/to/our/app/show
```

To post to the API, use the following line of code:

```
curl --data "name=Night+Court&year=1984" http://path/to/our/app/show
```

There's more...

Keep in mind that this API example is very basic. To make it better, we would need to add in some validation whenever we add or update a record. It would also be a good idea to add in some kind of authentication so that the public wouldn't be able to alter our table and delete records.

We could also use Laravel's resourceful controllers to accomplish something similar. More information about those can be found in the documentation at `http://laravel.com/docs/controllers#resource-controllers`.

Using named routes

There may be times when we need to change our route's name. On a large site, this could cause a lot of problems if we have multiple links to an incorrect route. Laravel provides an easy-to-use way of assigning names to our routes, so we never have to worry if they change.

Getting ready

For this recipe, we need a standard Laravel installation.

How to do it...

To complete this recipe, follow these steps:

1. In our `routes.php` file, create a named route as follows:

```
Route::get('main-route', array('as' => 'named', function()
{
    return 'Welcome to ' . URL::current();
}));
```

2. Create a route that performs a simple redirect to the named route:

```
Route::get('redirect', function()
{
    return Redirect::route('named');
});
```

3. Create a route that displays a link to the named route:

```
Route::get('link', function()
{
    return '<a href="' . URL::route('named') . '">Link!</a>';
});
```

4. In the browser, visit `http://your-server/redirect` and `http://your-server/link` (where `your-server` is the URL for the server) and notice that they send us to the `main-route` route.

5. Now, rename the `main-route` route to `new-route`:

```
Route::get('new-route', array('as' => 'named', function()
{
    return 'Welcome to ' . URL::current();
}));
```

6. In the browser, visit the **redirect** and **link** routes and see where they send us now.

How it works...

There may be times when your route will need to change; for example, if a client has a blog but wants the route "posts" to become "articles". If we have links to the "posts" route throughout our site, it would mean we need to find every file and make sure they're changed. By using a named route, we can rename the route to anything we want, and as long as all our links point to the name, everything will stay updated.

In our example, we have route `main-route` and have it named `named`. Now, if we want to link or redirect to the route, we can use `route()` pointing to the named route. Then, if we change the route to `new-route` and recheck those links, it will automatically go to the changed route.

Using a subdomain in your route

Many modern web applications offer customized content to their users, including giving them a custom subdomain where they can access their content. For example, instead of a user's profile page being `http://example.com/users/37`, we might want to offer `http://username.example.com`. By changing some DNS and Apache settings, we can easily provide the same functionality in Laravel.

Getting ready

For this recipe, we need access to our DNS settings and our server's Apache configurations. We'll also need a properly configured MySQL database and a standard Laravel installation. Throughout the recipe, we'll be using `example.com` as the domain name.

How to do it...

To complete this recipe, follow these steps:

1. In the DNS for our domain name, we need to add an "A" record using a wildcard for the subdomain, such as `*.example.com`, and then point it to our server's IP address.

2. Open up Apache's `httpd.conf` file and add a virtual host to it as follows:

```
<VirtualHost *:80>
  ServerName example.com
  ServerAlias *.example.com
</VirtualHost>
```

3. In the command line, go to our application route and create a migration for our `names` table:

```
php artisan migrate:make create_names_table
```

4. In the `migrations` directory, open the `create_names_table` file and add our schema:

```
<?php

use Illuminate\Database\Migrations\Migration;

class CreateNamesTable extends Migration {

    /**
```

```
     * Run the migrations.
     *
     * @return void
     */
    public function up()
    {
        Schema::create('users', function($table)
        {
            $table->increments('id');
            $table->string('name');
            $table->string('full_name');
            $table->timestamps();
        });
    }

    /**
     * Reverse the migrations.
     *
     * @return void
     */
    public function down()
    {
      Schema::drop('name');
    }
}
```

5. Back in the command line, create another migration to add some test data:

```
php artisan migrate:make add_names_data
```

6. Open the add_names_data file in the migrations directory:

```
<?php

use Illuminate\Database\Migrations\Migration;

class AddNamesData extends Migration {

  /**
   * Run the migrations.
   *
   * @return void
   */
  public function up()
  {
      $names = array(
```

```
                array(
                        'name' => 'bob',
                        'full_name' => 'Bob Smith'
                        ),
                        array(
                            'name' => 'carol',
                            'full_name' => 'Carol Smith'
                            ),
                        array(
                            'name' => 'ted',
                            'full_name' => 'Ted Jones'
                            )
                );
    DB::table('name')->insert($names);
}

/**
 * Reverse the migrations.
 *
 * @return void
 */
public function down()
{
    DB::table('name')->delete();
}
}
```

7. In the command line, run the migration as follows:

    ```
    php artisan migrate
    ```

8. Create a route to get information from the `names` table based on the subdomain:

    ```
    Route::get('/', function()
    {
      $url = parse_url(URL::all());
      $host = explode('.', $url['host']);
      $subdomain = $host[0];

      $name = DB::table('name')->where('name',$subdomain)-
      >get();

      dd($name);
    });
    ```

9. In the browser, visit our domain with a relevant subdomain such as
    `http://ted.example.com`.

How it works...

To start off, we need to update our DNS and our server. In our DNS, we create a wildcard subdomain and create a virtual host in our Apache configuration. This makes sure that any subdomains used will go to our main application.

For our default route, we use the `parse_url` function of PHP to get the domain name, explode it into an array, and use only the first element. We can then query the database using the subdomain and create a customized experience for the user.

There's more...

This recipe allows for a single route to process the subdomains, but if we would like to use more routes with a subdomain, we could use a route group similar to the following:

```
Route::group(array('domain' => '{subdomain}.myapp.com'), function()
{
    Route::get('/', function($subdomain)
    {
        $name = DB::table('name')->where('name', $subdomain)-
        >get();
      dd($name);

    });
});
```

6

Displaying Your Views

In this chapter, we will cover:

- ▸ Creating and using a basic view
- ▸ Passing data into a view
- ▸ Loading a view into another view/nested views
- ▸ Adding assets
- ▸ Creating a view using Blade
- ▸ Using TWIG templates
- ▸ Utilizing advanced Blade usage
- ▸ Creating localization of content
- ▸ Creating menus in Laravel
- ▸ Integrating with Bootstrap
- ▸ Using named views and view composers

Introduction

In a Model-View-Controller setup, our **views** hold all the HTML and styles so we can display our data. In Laravel, our views can use either regular PHP files or we can use Laravel's Blade templating. Laravel is also extensible enough to allow us to use any templating engine we may want to include.

Creating and using a basic view

In this recipe, we'll see some basic **view** functionality and how we can include views in our app.

Getting ready

For this recipe, we need a standard Laravel installation.

How to do it...

Follow these steps to complete the recipe:

1. In the app/views directory, create a folder name myviews.

2. In the new myviews directory, create two files: home.php and second.php.

3. Open home.php and add the following code in HTML:

```html
<!doctype html>
<html lang="en">
    <head>
        <meta charset="utf-8">
        <title>Home Page</title>
    </head>
    <body>
      <h1>Welcome to the Home page!</h1>
      <p>
        <a href="second">Go to Second Page</a>
      </p>
    </body>
</html>
```

4. Open the second.php file and add the following code in HTML:

```html
<!doctype html>
<html lang="en">
    <head>
        <meta charset="utf-8">
        <title>Second Page</title>
    </head>
    <body>
      <h1>Welcome to the Second Page</h1>
      <p>
        <a href="home">Go to Home Page</a>
      </p>
    </body>
</html>
```

5. In our `app/routes.php` file, add the routes that will return these views:

```
Route::get('home', function()
{
   return View::make('myviews.home');
});
Route::get('second', function()
{
   return View::make('myviews.second');
});
```

6. Test the views by going to `http://{your-server}/home` (where `your-server` is our URL) and clicking on the link.

How it works...

All of the views in Laravel are kept in the `app/views` directory. We start by creating two files that will hold our HTML. In this example, we're creating static pages, with each view holding its own full HTML markup.

In our routes file, we then return `View::make()`, with the name of the view passed in. Since our views are in a subdirectory of the views directory, we use the dot notation.

Passing data into a view

In our web app, we will usually need to display some kind of data from our database or other data store. In Laravel, we can easily pass that data into our views.

Getting ready

For this recipe, we need to have completed the *Creating and using a basic view* recipe .

How to do it...

To complete this recipe, follow these steps:

1. Open the `routes.php` and replace our home and second routes to include the following data:

```
Route::get('home', function()
{
   $page_title = 'My Home Page Title';
   return View::make('myviews.home')->with('title',
     $page_title);
});
```

```
Route::get('second', function()
{
  $view = View::make('myviews.second');
  $view->my_name = 'John Doe';
  $view->my_city = 'Austin';
  return $view;
});
```

2. In the `view/myviews` directory, open `home.php` and replace the code with the following code:

```html
<!doctype html>
<html lang="en">
    <head>
        <meta charset="utf-8">
        <title>Home Page : <?= $title ?></title>
    </head>
    <body>
        <h1>Welcome to the Home page!</h1>
        <h2><?= $title ?></h2>
      <p>
        <a href="second">Go to Second Page</a>
      </p>
    </body>
</html>
```

3. In the `views/myviews` directory, open the `second.php` file and replace the code with the following code:

```html
<!doctype html>
<html lang="en">
    <head>
        <meta charset="utf-8">
        <title>Second Page</title>
    </head>
    <body>
      <h1>Welcome to the Second Page</h1>
        <p> You are <?= $my_name ?>, from <?= $my_city ?>
        </p>
      <p>
        <a href="home">Go to Home Page</a>
      </p>
    </body>
</html>
```

4. Test the views by going to `http://{your-server}/home` (where `your-server` is our URL) and then clicking on the link.

How it works...

If we want to get data into our views, Laravel offers various ways to accomplish this. We start by updating our first route by passing a single variable to the view, by chaining the `with()` method to `View::make()`. Then, in the view file, we can access the variable by using whichever name we chose.

In our next route, we assign `View::make()` to a variable, and then assign values as the object's properties. We can then access those properties as variables in our view. To display the view, we simply return the object variable.

There's more...

One other way to add data to our views is similar to the way in our second route; however we use an array instead of an object. So our code would look similar to the following:

```
$view = View::make('myviews.second');
$view['my_name'] = 'John Doe';
$view['my_city'] = 'Austin';
return $view;
```

Loading a view into another view/nested views

Very often, our web pages will have a similar layout and HTML structure. To help separate out the repeated HTML, we can use **nested views** in Laravel.

Getting ready

For this recipe, we need to have completed the *Creating and using a basic view* recipe.

How to do it...

To complete this recipe, follow these steps:

1. In the `app/view` directory, add a new folder named `common`.

2. In the `common` directory, create a file named `header.php` and add the following code to it:

```
<!doctype html>
<html lang="en">
    <head>
        <meta charset="utf-8">
```

```
        <title>My Website</title>
    </head>
    <body>
```

3. In the `common` directory, create a file named `footer.php` and add the following code to it:

```
<footer>&copy; 2013 MyCompany</footer>
    </body>
</html>
```

4. In the `common` directory, create a file named `userinfo.php` and add the following code to it:

```
<p>You are <?= $my_name ?>, from <?= $my_city ?></p>
```

5. In the `routes.php` file, update the home and second route to include the following nested views:

```
Route::get('home', function()
{
    return View::make('myviews.home')
        ->nest('header', 'common.header')
        ->nest('footer', 'common.footer');
});
Route::get('second', function()
{
    $view = View::make('myviews.second');
    $view->nest('header', 'common.header')->nest('footer',
     'common.footer');
    $view->nest('userinfo', 'common.userinfo',
    array('my_name' => 'John Doe', 'my_city' => 'Austin'));
    return $view;
});
```

6. In the `views/myviews` directory, open the `home.php` file and add the following code to it:

```
<?= $header ?>
    <h1>Welcome to the Home page!</h1>
    <p>
        <a href="second">Go to Second Page</a>
    </p>
<?= $footer ?>
```

7. In the `views/myviews` directory, open the `second.php` file and add the following code to it:

```
<?= $header ?>
<h1>Welcome to the Second Page</h1>
  <?= $userinfo ?>
<p>
    <a href="home">Go to Home Page</a>
</p>
<?= $footer ?>
```

8. Test the views by going to `http://{your-server}/home` (where `your-server` is our URL) and then clicking on the link.

How it works...

To begin, we need to separate out our header and footer code from our views. Since these will be the same on every page, we create a subdirectory in our `views` folder to hold our common files. The first file is our header, which will hold everything up until the `<body>` tag. Our second file is our footer, which will hold the HTML at the bottom of our page.

Our third file is a `userinfo` view. Very often, if we have user accounts with profiles, we may want to include the user's data in a sidebar or header. So that we can keep that one piece of our view separate, we create the `userinfo` view with some data that we will pass to it.

For our home route, we will use our home view and nest in the header and footer. The first parameter in the `nest()` method is the name we will use in the main view and the second parameter is the location of the view. For this example, our views are on the common subdirectory, so we use the dot notation to reference them.

In our home view, to display the nested views, we print out the variable name we used in our route.

For our second route, we nest in the header and footer as well but we also want to add in the `userinfo` view. For this, we pass in a third parameter to the `nest()` method, which is an array of the data we want to send to the view. Then, in our main view, when we print out the `userinfo` view, it will automatically have the variables included.

See also

▶   The *Passing data into a view* recipe

Adding assets

A dynamic website almost requires the use of CSS and JavaScript. Using a Laravel asset package provides an easy way to manage these assets and include them in our views.

Getting ready

For this recipe, we'll need to use the code created in the *Loading a view into another view/ nested views* recipe.

How to do it...

To complete this recipe, follow these steps:

1. Open the `composer.json` file and add the `asset` package to the `require` section, so it looks similar to the following:

   ```
   "require": {
          "laravel/framework": "4.0.*",
          "teepluss/asset": "dev-master"
       },
   ```

2. In the command line, run composer update to download the package as follows:

   ```
   php composer.phar update
   ```

3. Open the `app/config/app.php` file and add `ServiceProvider` to the end of the providers array as follows:

   ```
   'Teepluss\Asset\AssetServiceProvider',
   ```

4. In the same file, in the `aliases` array, add the alias for the package as follows:

   ```
   'Asset' => 'Teepluss\Asset\Facades\Asset'
   ```

5. In the `app/filters.php` file, add a custom filter for our assets as follows:

   ```
   Route::filter('assets', function()
   {
     Asset::add('jqueryui', 'http://ajax.googleapis.com/ajax
       /libs/jqueryui/1.10.2/jquery-ui.min.js', 'jquery');
     Asset::add('jquery', 'http://ajax.googleapis.com/ajax
       /libs/jquery/1.10.2/jquery.min.js');
     Asset::add('bootstrap', 'http://netdna.bootstrapcdn.com
       /twitter-bootstrap/2.3.2/css/
       bootstrap-combined.min.css');
   });
   ```

Update the home and second routes to use the filter

```
Route::get('home', array('before' => 'assets', function()
{
    return View::make('myviews.home')
        ->nest('header', 'common.header')
        ->nest('footer', 'common.footer');
}));
Route::get('second', array('before' => 'assets', function()
{
    $view = View::make('myviews.second');
    $view->nest('header', 'common.header')->nest
    ('footer', 'common.footer');
    $view->nest('userinfo', 'common.userinfo', array
    ('my_name' => 'John Doe', 'my_city' => 'Austin'));
    return $view;
}));
```

6. In the `views/common` directory, open `header.php` and use this code as follows:

```
<!doctype html>
<html lang="en">
    <head>
        <meta charset="utf-8">
        <title>My Website</title>
        <?= Asset::styles() ?>
    </head>
    <body>
```

7. In the `views/common` directory, open `footer.php` and use the following code:

```
<footer>&copy; 2013 MyCompany</footer>
<?= Asset::scripts() ?>
    </body>
</html>
```

8. Test the views by going to `http://{your-server}/home` (where `your-server` is our URL), clicking on the link, and viewing the source of the page to see the assets included.

How it works...

The `asset` package makes it very easy to add CSS and JavaScript files to our HTML. To begin, we need to "register" each asset with the routes. To make things a bit simpler, we'll add the assets in a filter that will be called before our routes. That way, we only have the code in one place and making changes will be easy. For our purposes, we'll use jQuery, jQueryUI, and bootstrap CSS from a CDN source.

The first parameter of the `add()` method is the name we're giving the asset. The second parameter is the URL of the asset; it could either be a relative path or a full URL. The third, optional parameter is the dependency of the asset. In our example, jQueryUI requires that jQuery already be loaded, so we pass in the name of our jQuery asset in the third parameter.

We then update our routes to add the filter. If we add or remove any assets in our filter, it will automatically be reflected in each of our routes.

Since we're using nested views, we only need to add the assets to our header and footer views. Our CSS files are called by the `styles()` method and the JavaScript is called by the `scripts()` method. Laravel checks the file extensions of the assets and automatically puts them in the right place. If we look at the source code, we'll notice that Laravel has also made sure to add the jQuery script before jQueryUI, since we set it as a dependency.

See also

> ▸ The *Using a filter on the route* recipe in *Chapter 5, Using Controllers and Routes for URLs and APIs*

Creating a view using Blade

PHP has many templating libraries available and Laravel's Blade is one of the best. This recipe will show an easily extendable way to get up-and-running with Blade templates, and quickly.

Getting ready

For this recipe, we need a standard Laravel installation.

How to do it...

To complete this recipe, follow these steps:

1. In the `routes.php` file, create new routes for our pages as follows:

```
Route::get('blade-home', function()
{
    return View::make('blade.home');
});
Route::get('blade-second', function()
{
    return View::make('blade.second');
});
```

2. In the `views` directory, create a new folder named `layout`.

3. In the `views/layout` directory, create a file named `index.blade.php` and add the following code to it:

```
<!doctype html>
<html lang="en">
    <head>
        <meta charset="utf-8">
        <title>My Site</title>
    </head>
    <body>
    <h1>
    @section('page_title')
       Welcome to
    @show
    </h1>
    @yield('content')
    </body>
</html>
```

4. In the `views` directory, create a folder named `blade`.

5. In the `views/blade` directory, create a file named `home.blade.php` and add the following code to it:

```
@extends('layout.index')

@section('page_title')
   @parent
     Our Blade Home
@endsection

@section('content')
   <p>
     Go to {{ HTML::link('blade-second',
     'the Second Page.') }}
   </p>
@endsection
```

6. In the `views/blade` directory, create a file named `second.blade.php`, and add the following code to it:

```
@extends('layout.index')

@section('page_title')
   @parent
     Our Second Blade Page
@endsection
```

```
@section('content')
  <p>
    Go to {{ HTML::link('blade-home', 'the Home Page.')
    }}
  </p>
@endsection
```

7. Test the views by going to `http://{your-server}/blade-home` (where `your-server` is our URL) and then clicking on the link, and viewing the source of the page to see the Blade layout included.

How it works...

To start, we create two simple routes that will return our Blade views. By using the dot notation, we can see that we'll be putting the files in the `blade` subdirectory of our `views` folder.

Our next step is to create a Blade layout view. This will be the skeleton of our pages and will be put in the layout subdirectory of our `views` folder, and it must have `blade.php` as the file extension. This view is simple HTML, with two exceptions: the `@section()` and `@yield()` areas. This content is what will be replaced or added to in our views.

In our routes' views, we begin the file by declaring which Blade layout to use, which for our case is `@extends('layout.index')`. Then we can add and alter the content sections we declared in our layout. For the `page_title` section, we want to display the text in the layout, but we want to add in some extra text to the end. To accomplish that, we call `@parent` as the first thing in that content area, and then put in any of our own content.

In `@section('content')`, there was no default text in the layout, so everything will be added. Using Blade, we can also use the `{{ }}` braces to print out any PHP we need. In our case, we're using the `HTML::link()` of Laravel to display a link. Now, when we go to the page, all the content area is put in the correct place in the layout.

Using TWIG templates

Laravel's Blade templates may be nice but there are times when we need another PHP template library. A popular one is Twig. This recipe will show how to incorporate Twig templates into our Laravel application.

Getting ready

For this recipe, we'll just need a standard Laravel installation.

How to do it...

Follow these steps to complete this recipe:

1. Open the `composer.json` file and add the following line to the `require` section:

   ```
   "rcrowe/twigbridge": "0.4.*"
   ```

2. In the command line, update composer to install the package:

   ```
   php composer.phar update
   ```

3. Open the `app/config/app.php` file and, in the `providers` array, add Twig ServiceProvider at the end as follows:

   ```
   'TwigBridge\TwigServiceProvider'
   ```

4. In the command line, run the following command to create our config file:

   ```
   php artisan config:publish rcrowe/twigbridge
   ```

5. In `routes.php`, create a route as follows:

   ```
   Route::get('twigview', function()
   {
     $link = HTML::link('http://laravel.com',
       'the Laravel site.');
     return View::make('twig')->with('link', $link);
   });
   ```

6. In the `views` directory, create a file named `twiglayout.twig` and add the following code to it:

   ```
   <!doctype html>
   <html lang="en">
       <head>
           <meta charset="utf-8">
           <title>My Site</title>
       </head>
       <body>
       <h1>
           {% block page_title %}
               Welcome to
           {% endblock %}
       </h1>
       {% block content %}{% endblock %}
       </body>
   </html>
   ```

7. In the `views` directory, create a file named `twig.twig`, and add the following code to it:

```
{% extends "twiglayout.twig" %}

{% block page_title %}
        {{ parent() }}
        My Twig Page
{% endblock %}

{% block content %}
    <p>
            Go to {{ link|raw }}
    </p>
{% endblock %}
```

8. Test the views by going to `http://your-server/twigview` (where `your-server` is our URL) and view the source of the page to see the twig layout included.

How it works...

To start, we're going to install the `TwigBranch` package into our application. This package also installs the `Twig` library. After the package is installed, we create its configuration file using `artisan`, and add its service provider.

In our route, we'll use the same syntax as Laravel's built-in view library, and call view. We're also creating a simple link, saving it to a variable, and passing that variable into the view.

Next, we create our layout. All Twig view files must have the `.twig` extension, so our layout is named `twiglayout.twig`. Inside the layout is a standard HTML skeleton, but we've added two Twig content blocks. The `page_title` block has some default content, while the `content` block is empty.

For our route's view, we begin by extending the layout view. For our `page_title` block, we start by printing out the default by using `{{ parent() }}` and then adding in our own content. Then our content block is added and will display the link we passed in as a variable. Using Twig, we don't need to use `$` for our variables, and if we pass in HTML, Twig will automatically escape it. So in our view, since we want to display the link, we need to make sure to add in the raw parameter.

Now, if we go to our page in the browser, we'll see all our content in its correct place.

Utilizing advanced Blade usage

Using Laravel's Blade templating system, we have access to some powerful features that make our development much quicker. For this recipe, we'll pass some data to our blade views and loop through it, along with some conditionals.

Getting ready

For this recipe, we'll need the code created in the *Creating a view using Blade* recipe .

How to do it...

Follow these steps to complete this recipe:

1. Open the `routes.php` file and update the `blade-home` and `blade-second` routes as follows:

```php
Route::get('blade-home', function()
{
  $movies = array(
    array('name' => 'Star Wars', 'year' => '1977', 'slug'
      => 'star-wars'),
    array('name' => 'The Matrix', 'year' => '1999',
      'slug' => 'matrix'),
    array('name' => 'Die Hard', 'year' => '1988', 'slug'
      => 'die-hard'),
    array('name' => 'Clerks', 'year' => '1994', 'slug'
      => 'clerks')
  );
  return View::make('blade.home')->with('movies',
    $movies);
});
Route::get('blade-second/(:any)', function($slug)
{
  $movies = array(
    'star-wars' => array('name' => 'Star Wars', 'year'
      => '1977', 'genre' => 'Sci-Fi'),
    'matrix' => array('name' => 'The Matrix', 'year'
      => '1999', 'genre' => 'Sci-Fi'),
    'die-hard' => array('name' => 'Die Hard', 'year'
      => '1988', 'genre' => 'Action'),
    'clerks' => array('name' => 'Clerks', 'year'
      => '1994', 'genre' => 'Comedy')
  );
  return View::make('blade.second')->with('movie'
    , $movies[$slug]);
});
```

2. In the `views/blade` directory, update the `home.blade.php` file with the following code:

```
@extends('layout.index')

@section('page_title')
  @parent
    Our List of Movies
@endsection

@section('content')
  <ul>
    @foreach ($movies as $movie)
      <li>{{ HTML::link('blade-second/' . $movie['slug'],
        $movie['name']) }} ( {{ $movie['year'] }} )</li>
        @if ($movie['name'] == 'Die Hard')
            <ul>
              <li>Main character: John McClane</li>
            </ul>
        @endif
    @endforeach
  </ul>
@endsection
```

3. In the `views/blade` directory, update the `second.blade.php` file with the following code:

```
@extends('layout.index')

@section('page_title')
  @parent
    Our {{ $movie['name'] }} Page
@endsection

@section('content')
  @include('blade.info')
  <p>
    Go to {{ HTML::link('blade-home', 'the Home Page.')
    }}
  </p>
@endsection
```

4. In the `views/blade` directory, create a new file named `info.blade.php` and add the following code to it:

```
<h1>{{ $movie['name'] }}</h1>
<p>Year: {{ $movie['year'] }}</p>
<p>Genre: {{ $movie['genre'] }}</p>
```

5. Test the views by going to `http://{your-server}/blade-home` (where `your-server` is our URL) and click on the links to see the views work.

How it works...

For this recipe, we'll be passing some data to our Blade views, looping through it, and adding in some conditionals. Typically, we would use this with results from a database but, for our purposes, we'll create a simple data array in our routes.

Our first route contains an array of movies, with their year and a slug that we can use for the URL. Our second route will create an array with the slug as a key and accept the slug in the URL. We then pass in the details of a single movie into the view, by calling the movie that has the slug as a key.

In our first view, we create a `@foreach` loop, to run through also the data in the array. We've also included a simple `@if` statement that checks for a specific movie and then prints out some extra information. As we loop through, we display links to the second route, with the slug added on.

The second view displays the name of the movie, but all includes another Blade view by using `@include()` in the content block. This way, all the data is also available in the included view; thus, for our `info` view, we can just use the same variables that we set in our route.

Creating localization of content

If our app is going to be used by people in different countries, or who speak different languages, we'll need to localize the content. Laravel provides an easy way to do this.

Getting ready

For this recipe, we just need a standard installation of Laravel.

How to do it...

For this recipe, follow these steps:

1. In the `app/lang` directory, add three new directories (if they aren't already there) : en, es, and de.

2. In the en directory, create a file named `localized.php` and add the following code to it:

```php
<?php

return array(
  'greeting' => 'Good morning :name',
  'meetyou' => 'Nice to meet you!',
  'goodbye' => 'Goodbye, see you tomorrow.',
);
```

3. In the es directory, create a file named `localized.php` and add the following code to it:

```php
<?php

return array(
   'greeting' => 'Buenos días :name',
   'meetyou' => 'Mucho gusto!',
   'goodbye' => 'Adiós, hasta mañana.',
);
```

4. In the de directory, create a file named `localized.php` and add the following code to it:

```php
<?php

return array(
   'greeting' => 'Guten morgen :name',
   'meetyou' => 'Es freut mich!',
   'goodbye' => 'Tag. Bis bald.',
);
```

5. In our `routes.php` file, create four routes as follows:

```php
Route::get('choose', function()
{
   return View::make('language.choose');
});
Route::post('choose', function()
{
   Session::put('lang', Input::get('language'));
   return Redirect::to('localized');
});
Route::get('localized', function()
{
   $lang = Session::get('lang', function() { return 'en';
    });
   App::setLocale($lang);
   return View::make('language.localized');
});
Route::get('localized-german', function()
{
   App::setLocale('de');
   return View::make('language.localized-german');
});
```

6. In the `views` directory, create a folder named `language`.

7. In `views/language`, create the file `choose.php` and add the following code to it:

```
<h2>Choose a Language:</h2>
<?= Form::open() ?>
<?= Form::select('language', array('en' => 'English', 'es' =>
'Spanish')) ?>
<?= Form::submit() ?>
<?= Form::close() ?>
```

8. In the `views/language` directory, create a file named `localized.php` and add the following code to it:

```
<h2>
  <?= Lang::get('localized.greeting', array('name' =>
  'Lindsay Weir')) ?>
</h2>
<p>
  <?= Lang::get('localized.meetyou') ?>
</p>
<p>
  <?= Lang::get('localized.goodbye') ?>
</p>
<p>
  <?= HTML::link('localized-german', 'Page 2') ?>
</p>
```

9. In the `views/language` directory, create a file named `localized-german.php` and add the following code to it:

```
<h2>
  <?= Lang::get('localized.greeting', array('name' =>
  'Lindsay Weir')) ?>
</h2>
<p>
  <?= Lang::get('localized.meetyou') ?>
</p>
<p>
  <?= Lang::get('localized.goodbye') ?>
</p>
```

10. In the browser, go to `http://{your-server}/choose` (where `your-server` is our URL), submit the form, and test the localization.

How it works...

For this recipe, we begin by setting up our language directories in the `app/lang` directory. We'll be using `en` for our English files, `es` for our Spanish files, and `de` for our German files. Inside each directory, we create a file using the exact same name, and add in an array, using the exact same keys.

Our first route is going to be a language selector page. On this page, we can choose either English or Spanish. When we submit, it will POST to the route, create a new session, add the choice, and redirect to the page to display the text in the chosen language.

Our localized route takes the session and passes the choice to App::setLocale(). We also have a default value of English if there was no session set.

In our localized view, we print out the text using Lang::get(). In the first line of our language file, we also included the :name placeholder, so we can pass in an array with the placeholder name as the key when we call the language file.

Our last route shows how we can statically set the language default in our route.

Creating menus in Laravel

Menus are a common facet of most websites. In this recipe, we'll create menus using Laravel's nested views and change the default "state" of the menu item, depending on which page we're on.

Getting ready

For this menu, we need a standard installation of Laravel.

How to do it...

We need to follow these steps to complete the recipe:

1. In the routes.php file, create three routes as follows:

```
Route::get('menu-one', function()
{
  return View::make('menu-layout')
      ->nest('menu', 'menu-menu')
      ->nest('content', 'menu-one');
});
Route::get('menu-two', function()
{
  return View::make('menu-layout')
      ->nest('menu', 'menu-menu')
      ->nest('content', 'menu-two');
});
Route::get('menu-three', function()
{
  return View::make('menu-layout')
      ->nest('menu', 'menu-menu')
      ->nest('content', 'menu-three');
});
```

2. In the views directory, create a file named menu-layout.php and add the following code to it:

```html
<!doctype html>
<html lang="en">
    <head>
        <meta charset="utf-8">
        <title>Menu Example</title>
        <style>
            #container {
                width: 1024px;
                margin: 0 auto;
                border-left: 2px solid #ddd;
                border-right: 2px solid #ddd;
                padding: 20px;
            }
            #menu { padding: 0 }
            #menu li {
                display: inline-block;
                border: 1px solid #ddf;
                border-radius: 6px;
                margin-right: 12px;
                padding: 4px 12px;
            }
            #menu li a {
                text-decoration: none;
                color: #069;
            }
            #menu li a:hover { text-decoration: underline
            }
            #menu li.active { background: #069 }
            #menu li.active a { color: #fff }
        </style>
    </head>
    <body>
      <div id="container">
          <?= $menu ?>
          <?= $content ?>
      </div>
    </body>
</html>
```

3. In the `views` directory, create a file named `menu-menu.php` and add the following code to it:

```html
<ul id="menu">
  <li class="<?= Request::segment(1) == 'menu-one' ?
    'active' : '' ?>">
```

```
        <?= HTML::link('menu-one', 'Page One') ?>
    </li>
    <li class="<?= Request::segment(1) == 'menu-two' ?
     'active' : '' ?>">
        <?= HTML::link('menu-two', 'Page Two') ?>
    </li>
    <li class="<?= Request::segment(1) == 'menu-three' ?
      'active' : '' ?>">
        <?= HTML::link('menu-three', 'Page Three') ?>
    </li>
</ul>
```

4. In the `views` directory, create three view files with the names `menu-one.php`, `menu-two.php`, and `menu-three.php`.

5. For `menu-one.php`, use the following code:

```
<h2>Page One</h2>
<p>
    Lorem ipsum dolor sit amet.
</p>
```

6. For `menu-two.php`, use the following code:

```
<h2>Page Two</h2>
<p>
    Suspendisse eu porta turpis
</p>
```

7. For `menu-three.php`, use the following code:

```
<h2>Page Three</h2>
<p>
    Nullam varius ultrices varius.
</p>
```

8. In the browser, go to `http://{your-server}/menu-one` (where `your-server` is our URL) and click through the menu links.

How it works...

We begin by making three routes to hold our three pages. Each route will use a single layout view, and nest in a menu view and a content view that are specific to the route.

Our layout view is a basic HTML skeleton with some on-page CSS. Since we want to highlight the menu item of the current page, one of the class selectors is named `active` and will be added to our menu list item.

Next, we create our menu view. We're using an unordered list, with links to each page. To add in the `active` class to our current page item, we use `Request::segment(1)` of Laravel to get the route we're on. If it's the same as the list item, we add the `active` class and otherwise leave it blank. Then we use the `HTML::link()` of Laravel to add in the links to our pages.

The other three views are just very simple content, with a header and a few words. Now, when we go to the page in our browser, we'll see the menu item of the page we're on is highlighted, while the others are not. If we click on a link, that item will then be highlighted and the others will not.

Integrating with Bootstrap

The Bootstrap CSS framework has become very popular recently. This recipe will show how we can use the framework with Laravel.

Getting ready

For this recipe, we need a standard Laravel installation. We'll also need to have the `assets` package installed, as demonstrated in the *Adding assets* recipe. Optionally, we could download the Bootstrap files and save them locally.

How to do it...

To complete this recipe, follow these steps:

1. In the `routes.php` file, create a new route as follows:

```
Route::any('boot', function()
{
  Asset::add('jquery', 'http://ajax.googleapis.com/ajax
    /libs/jquery/1.10.2/jquery.min.js');
  Asset::add('bootstrap-js', 'http://
    netdna.bootstrapcdn.com/twitter-
    bootstrap/2.3.2/js/bootstrap.min.js', 'jquery');
  Asset::add('bootstrap-css', 'http://
    netdna.bootstrapcdn.com/twitter-
    bootstrap/2.3.2/css/bootstrap-combined.min.css');
  $superheroes = array('Batman', 'Superman', 'Wolverine',
    'Deadpool', 'Iron Man');
  return View::make('boot')->with('superheroes',
    $superheroes);
});
```

2. In the `views` directory, create a file named `boot.php` add the following code to it:

```php
<!doctype html>
<html lang="en">
  <head>
    <meta charset="utf-8">
    <title>My Bootstrap Page</title>
    <?= Asset::styles() ?>
  </head>
  <body>
    <div class="container">
      <h1>Using Bootstrap with Laravel</h1>
      <ul class="nav nav-tabs">
        <li class="active"><a href="#welcome" data-
        toggle="tab">Welcome</a></li>
        <li><a href="#about" data-toggle="tab">
        About Us</a></li>
        <li><a href="#contact" data-toggle="tab">
        Contact</a></li>
      </ul>
        <div class="tab-content">
          <div class="tab-pane active" id="welcome">
            <h4>Welcome to our site</h4>
            <p>Here's a list of Superheroes:</p>
            <ul>
              <?php foreach($superheroes as $hero): ?>
                <li class="badge badge-info">
                <?= $hero ?></li>
              <?php endforeach; ?>
            </ul>
      </div>
          <div class="tab-pane" id="about">
            <h4>About Us</h4>
              <p>Cras at dui eros. Ut imperdiet
                pellentesque mi faucibus dapibus.
                Phasellus vitae lacus at massa viverra
                condimentum quis quis augue. Etiam
                pharetra erat id sem pretium egestas.
                Suspendisse mollis, dolor a sagittis
                hendrerit, urna velit commodo dui, id
                adipiscing magna magna ac ligula. Nunc
                in ligula nunc.</p>
          </div>
          <div class="tab-pane" id="contact">
            <h3>Contact Form</h3>
              <?= Form::open('boot', 'POST') ?>
                <?= Form::label('name', 'Your Name') ?>
                <?= Form::text('name') ?>
```

```
<?= Form::label('email', 'Your Email') ?>
<?= Form::text('email') ?>
<br>
<?= Form::button('Send', array('class' =>
 'btn btn-primary')) ?>

<?= Form::close() ?>
        </div>
      </div>
    </div>
    <?= Asset::scripts() ?>
  </body>
</html>
```

3. In the browser, go to `http://your-server/boot` (where `your-server` is our URL) and click through the tabs.

How it works...

For this recipe, we'll be creating a single route and switch content using Bootstrap tabs. To get our route to respond to any request, we use `Route::any()` and pass in our closure. To add in the CSS and JavaScript, we could use a filter as with in the one in the *Adding assets* recipe; however, for a single route, we'll just include it in the closure. So we don't have to download them, we'll just use the CDN versions of Bootstrap and jQuery.

Next in our route, we need some data. This would be a good place to tie in a database but, for our purposes, we'll use a simple array, with the names of some super heroes. We then pass that array into our view.

We start the view with an HTML skeleton and include our styles in the head and the scripts just before the closing `</body>` tag. At the top of the page, we use Bootstrap's navigation styles and data attributes to create our tab links. Then in our body, we use three different tab panes, with IDs that correspond to the `<a href>` tag in our menu.

When we view the page, we'll see the first pane showing and everything else hidden. By clicking on the other tabs, we switch which tab pane is shown.

See also

▶ The *Adding assets* recipe

Using named views and view composers

This recipe will show how to use Laravel's named views and view composers to simplify some of our routes' code.

Getting ready

For this recipe, we'll be using the code created in the *Creating menus in Laravel* recipe. We'll also need the `assets` package installed in the *Adding assets* recipe.

How to do it...

To complete this recipe, follow these steps:

1. In the `routes.php` file, add a file named `view`, and add the following code to it:

   ```
   View::name('menu-layout', 'layout');
   ```

2. In `routes.php`, add a view composer as follows:

   ```
   View::composer('menu-layout', function($view)
   {
     Asset::add('bootstrap-css',
      'http://netdna.bootstrapcdn.com/twitter-
       bootstrap/2.2.2/css/bootstrap-combined.min.css');
       $view->nest('menu', 'menu-menu');
       $view->with('page_title', 'View Composer Title');
   });
   ```

3. In `routes.php`, update the menu routes as follows:

   ```
   Route::get('menu-one', function()
   {
     return View::of('layout')->nest('content', 'menu-one');
   });
   Route::get('menu-two', function()
   {
     return View::of('layout')->nest('content', 'menu-two');
   });
   Route::get('menu-three', function()
   {
     return View::of('layout')->nest('content', 'menu-three');
   });
   ```

4. In the `views` directory, update the `menu-layout.php` file with the following code:

```php
<!doctype html>
<html lang="en">
    <head>
        <meta charset="utf-8">
        <title><?= $page_title ?></title>
        <?= Asset::styles() ?>
        <style>
          #container {
             width: 1024px;
             margin: 0 auto;
             border-left: 2px solid #ddd;
             border-right: 2px solid #ddd;
             padding: 20px;
          }
          #menu { padding: 0 }
          #menu li {
             display: inline-block;
             border: 1px solid #ddf;
             border-radius: 6px;
             margin-right: 12px;
             padding: 4px 12px;
          }
          #menu li a {
             text-decoration: none;
             color: #069;
          }
          #menu li a:hover { text-decoration: underline }
          #menu li.active { background: #069 }
          #menu li.active a { color: #fff }
        </style>
    </head>
    <body>
      <div id="container">
        <?= $menu ?>
        <?= $content ?>
      </div>
    </body>
</html>
```

5. In the browser, go to `http://{your-server}/menu-one` (where `your-server` is our URL) and click through the menu links.

How it works...

We begin the recipe by creating a name for one of our views. If we have views with long or complicated filenames or directory structures, this will allow us to create a simple alias in our routes. It will also let us change our view filename in the future; additionally, if we're using it in more than one place, we only need to change one line.

Next, we create a view composer. Any code in the composer will automatically be called when you create the view. In our example, we're including three things every time our view is created: an asset containing a Bootstrap CSS file, a nested view, and a variable to pass to the view.

For our three routes, instead of `View::make('menu-layout')`, we'll use the name we created, call `View::of('layout')`, and nest it in our content. Since our layout view has a composer, it will automatically nest in our menu, add the CSS, and pass in a page title.

See also

▶ The *Creating menus in Laravel* recipe

7
Creating and Using Composer Packages

In this chapter, we will cover:

- ► Downloading and installing packages
- ► Using the Generators package to set up an app
- ► Creating a Composer package in Laravel
- ► Adding your Composer package to Packagist
- ► Adding a non-Packagist package to Composer
- ► Creating a custom artisan command

Introduction

One of the great features in Laravel is the ease in which we can include the class libraries that others have made using bundles. On the Laravel site, there are already many useful bundles, some of which automate certain tasks while others easily integrate with third-party APIs.

A recent addition to the PHP world is Composer, which allows us to use libraries (or packages) that aren't specific to Laravel.

In this chapter, we'll get up-and-running with using bundles, and we'll even create our own bundle that others can download. We'll also see how to incorporate Composer into our Laravel installation to open up a wide range of PHP libraries that we can use in our application.

Downloading and installing packages

One of the best features of Laravel is how modular it is. Most of the framework is built using libraries, or **packages**, that are well tested and widely used in other projects. By using Composer for dependency management, we can easily include other packages and seamlessly integrate them into our Laravel app.

For this recipe, we'll be installing two popular packages into our app: Jeffrey Way's Laravel 4 Generators and the `Imagine` image processing packages.

Getting ready

For this recipe, we need a standard installation of Laravel using Composer.

How to do it...

For this recipe, we will follow these steps:

1. Go to `https://packagist.org/`.

2. In the search box, search for `way generator` as shown in the following screenshot:

3. Click on the link for **way/generators**:

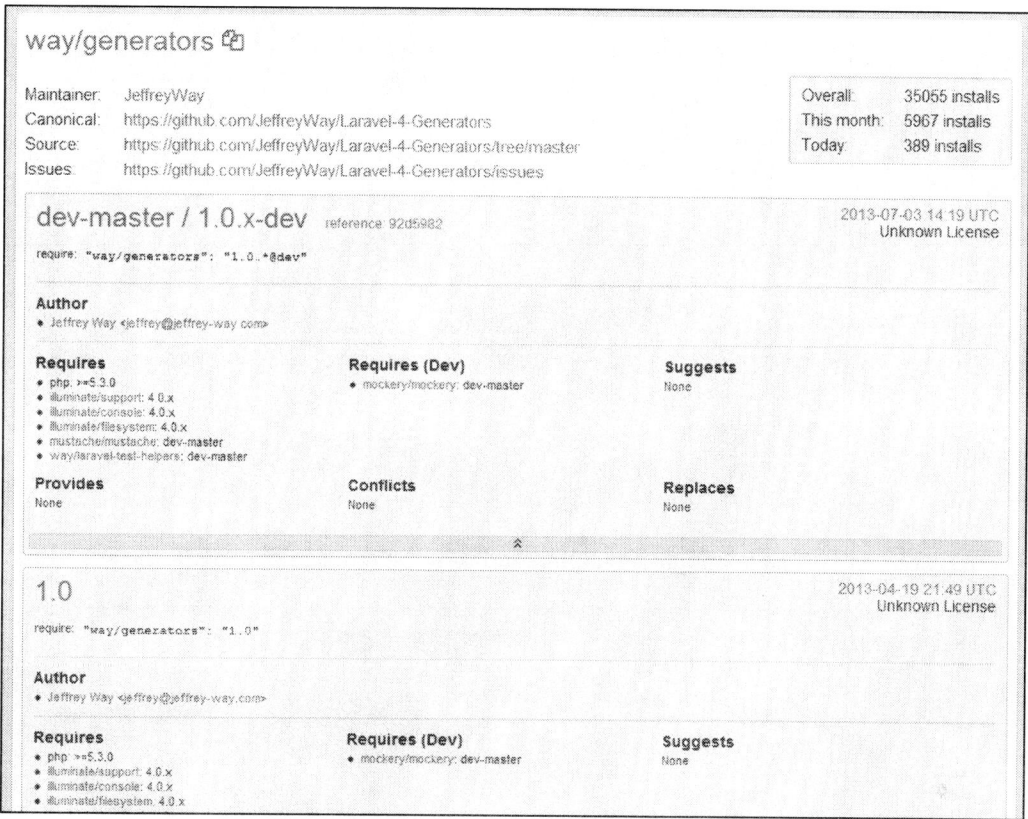

4. View the details at `https://packagist.org/packages/way/generators` and take notice of the **require** line to get the package's version. For our purposes, we'll use **"way/generators": "1.0.*"**.

5. In our application's root directory, open up the `composer.json` file and add in the package to the `require` section so it looks like this:

```
"require": {
        "laravel/framework": "4.0.*",
        "way/generators": "1.0.*"
},
```

6. Go back to `http://packagist.org` and perform a search for `imagine` as shown in the following screenshot:

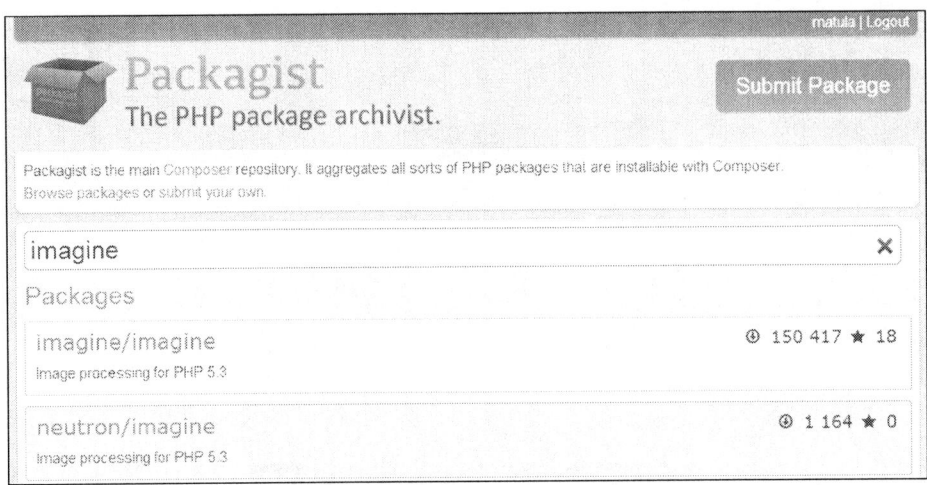

7. Click on the link to **imagine/imagine** and copy the require code for **dev-master**:

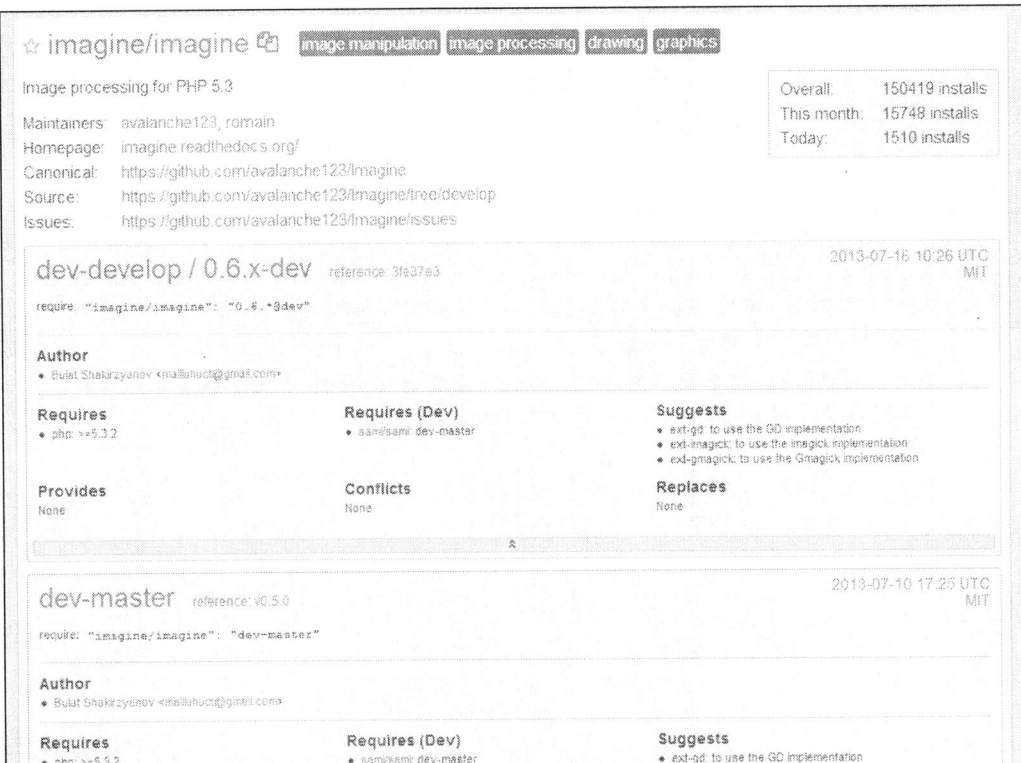

8. Go back to our `composer.json` file and update the `require` section to include the `imagine` package . It should now look similar to the following code:

    ```
    "require": {
            "laravel/framework": "4.0.*",
            "way/generators": "1.0.*",
            "imagine/imagine": "dev-master"
    },
    ```

9. Open the command line, and in the root of our application, run the Composer update as follows:

    ```
    php composer.phar update
    ```

10. Finally, we'll add the Generator Service Provider, so open the `app/config/app.php` file and in the providers array, add the following line:

    ```
    'Way\Generators\GeneratorsServiceProvider'
    ```

How it works...

To get our package, we first go to `packagist.org` and search for the package we want. We could also click on the **Browse packages** link. It will display a list of the most recent packages as well as the most popular. After clicking on the package we want, we'll be taken to the detail page, which lists various links including the package's repository and home page. We could also click on the package's maintainer link to see other packages they have released.

Underneath, we'll see the various versions of the package. If we open that version's detail page, we'll find the code we need to use for our `composer.json` file. We could either choose to use a strict version number, add a wildcard to the version, or use `dev-master`, which will install whatever is updated on the package's master branch. For the `Generators` package, we'll only use Version 1.0, but allow any minor fixes to that version. For the `imagine` package, we'll use `dev-master`, so whatever is in their repository's master branch will be downloaded, regardless of version number.

We then run update on Composer and it will automatically download and install all of the packages we chose. Finally, to use `Generators` in our app, we need to register the service provider in our app's config file.

Using the Generators package to set up an app

`Generators` is a popular Laravel package that automates quite a bit of file creation. In addition to `controllers` and `models`, it can also generate `views`, `migrations`, `seeds`, and more, all through a command-line interface.

Getting ready

For this recipe, we'll be using the Laravel 4 Generators package maintained by *Jeffrey Way* that was installed in the *Downloading and installing packages* recipe. We'll also need a properly configured MySQL database.

How to do it...

Follow these steps for this recipe:

1. Open the command line in the root of our app and, using the generator, create a scaffold for our cities as follows:

   ```
   php artisan generate:scaffold cities --fields="city:string"
   ```

2. In the command line, create a scaffold for our superheroes as follows:

   ```
   php artisan generate:scaffold superheroes --fields="name:string,
   city_id:integer:unsigned"
   ```

3. In our project, look in the app/database/seeds directory and find a file named CitiesTableSeeder.php. Open it and add some data to the $cities array as follows:

   ```php
   <?php

   class CitiesTableSeeder extends Seeder {

     public function run()
     {
       DB::table('cities')->delete();

       $cities = array(
           array(
                   'id'         => 1,
                   'city'       => 'New York',
                   'created_at' => date('Y-m-d g:i:s',
                     time())
               ),
           array(
                   'id'         => 2,
                   'city'       => 'Metropolis',
                   'created_at' => date('Y-m-d g:i:s',
                     time())
               ),
           array(
                   'id'         => 3,
                   'city'       => 'Gotham',
                   'created_at' => date('Y-m-d g:i:s',
                     time())
   ```

```
              )
      );

      DB::table('cities')->insert($cities);
    }
}
```

4. In the app/database/seeds directory, open SuperheroesTableSeeder.php and add some data to it:

```php
<?php

class SuperheroesTableSeeder extends Seeder {

  public function run()
  {
    DB::table('superheroes')->delete();

      $superheroes = array(
          array(
                  'name'       => 'Spiderman',
                  'city_id'    => 1,
                  'created_at' => date('Y-m-d g:i:s',
                    time())
                  ),
          array(
                  'name'       => 'Superman',
                  'city_id'    => 2,
                  'created_at' => date('Y-m-d g:i:s',
                    time())
                  ),
          array(
                  'name'       => 'Batman',
                  'city_id'    => 3,
                  'created_at' => date('Y-m-d g:i:s',
                    time())
                  ),
          array(
                  'name'       => 'The Thing',
                  'city_id'    => 1,
                  'created_at' => date('Y-m-d g:i:s',
                    time())
                  )
        );

    DB::table('superheroes')->insert($superheroes);
  }
}
```

5. In the command line, run the migration then seed the database as follows:

    ```
    php artisan migrate
    php artisan db:seed
    ```

6. Open up a web browser and go to `http://{your-server}/cities`. We will see our data as shown in the following screenshot:

7. Now, navigate to `http://{your-server}/superheroes` and we will see our data as shown in the following screenshot:

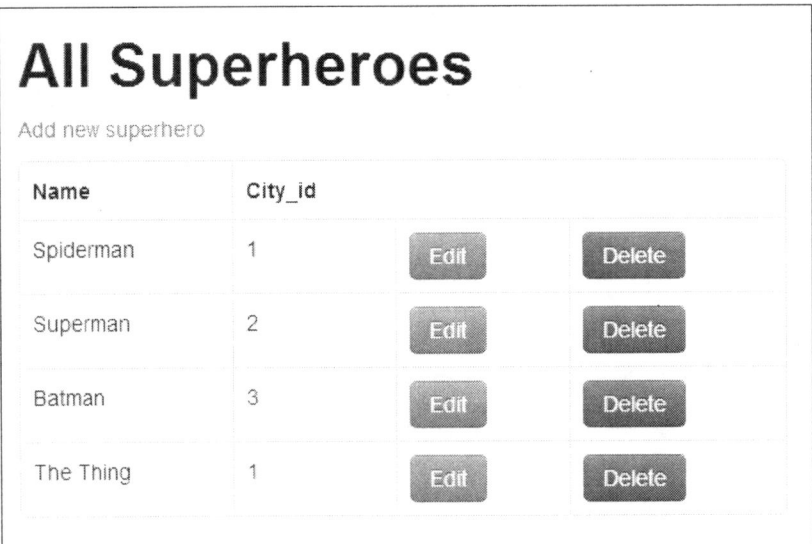

How it works...

We begin by running the scaffold generator for our cities and superheroes tables. Using the `--fields` tag, we can determine which columns we want in our table and also set options such as data type. For our cities table, we'll only need the name of the city. For our superheroes table, we'll want the name of the hero as well as the ID of the city where they live.

When we run the generator, many files will automatically be created for us. For example, with cities, we'll get `City.php` in our models, `CitiesController.php` in controllers, and a `cities` directory in our views with the index, show, create, and edit views. We then get a migration named `Create_cities_table.php`, a `CitiesTableSeeder.php` seed file, and `CitiesTest.php` in our `tests` directory. We'll also have our `DatabaseSeeder.php` file and our `routes.php` file updated to include everything we need.

To add some data to our tables, we opened the `CitiesTableSeeder.php` file and updated our `$cities` array with arrays that represent each row we want to add. We did the same thing for our `SuperheroesTableSeeder.php` file. Finally, we run the migrations and seeder and our database will be created and all the data will be inserted.

The `Generators` package has already created the views and controllers we need to manipulate the data, so we can easily go to our browser and see all of our data. We can also create new rows, update existing rows, and delete rows.

Creating a Composer package in Laravel

Using Laravel's Workbench, we can easily create a package that can be used and installed by Composer. We can also add functionality so that the package integrates seamlessly into our Laravel app. In this recipe, we'll be creating a simple package that will display a list of Vimeo videos for a specified user.

Getting ready

For this recipe, we'll need a standard Laravel installation.

How to do it...

To complete this recipe, follow these steps:

1. In the app/config directory, open the workbench.php file and update it with the following information:

```php
<?php

return array(

    'name' => 'Terry Matula',

    'email' => 'terrymatula@gmail.com',

);
```

2. In the command line, use artisan to set up our package:

```
php artisan workbench matula/vimeolist --resources
```

3. Find the directory that will hold our source files and create a file named Vimeolist. php. In this example, we would put the file in workbench/matula/vimeolist/ src/Matula/Vimeolist/:

```php
<?php namespace Matula\Vimeolist;

class Vimeolist
{
  private $base_url =
  'http://vimeo.com/api/v2/{username}/videos.json';
  private $username;

  public function __construct($username = 'userscape') {
      $this->setUser($username);
      return $this;
  }

  /**
   * Set the username for our list
   *
   * @return void
   */
  public function setUser($username = NULL) {
      $this->username = is_null($username) ? $this-
      >username : urlencode($username);
       return $this;
  }
```

```php
/**
 * Set up the url and get the contents
 *
 * @return json
 */
private function getFeed() {
    $url  = str_replace('{username}', $this->username,
    $this->base_url);
    $feed = file_get_contents($url);
    return $feed;
}


/**
 * Turn the feed into an object
 *
 * @return object
 */
public function parseFeed() {
    $json = $this->getFeed();
    $object = json_decode($json);
    return $object;
}


/**
 * Get the list and format the return
 *
 * @return array
 */
public function getList() {
    $list = array();
    $posts = $this->parseFeed();
    foreach ($posts as $post) {
            $list[$post->id]['title']    = $post->title;
            $list[$post->id]['url']      = $post->url;
            $list[$post->id]['description'] = $post-
              >description;
            $list[$post->id]['thumbnail'] = $post-
              >thumbnail_small;
    }
    return $list;
}
}
```

4. In the same directory as the file we just created, open the file named
    `VimeolistServiceProvider.php` and update it:

```php
<?php namespace Matula\Vimeolist;

use Illuminate\Support\ServiceProvider;

class VimeolistServiceProvider extends ServiceProvider {

    /**
     * Indicates if loading of the provider is deferred.
     *
     * @var bool
     */
    protected $defer = false;

    /**
     * Bootstrap the application events.
     *
     * @return void
     */
    public function boot()
    {
        $this->package('matula/vimeolist');
    }

    /**
     * Register the service provider.
     *
     * @return void
     */
    public function register()
    {
        $this->app['vimeolist'] = $this->app-
          >share(function($app)
              {
                return new Vimeolist;
              });
    }

    /**
     * Get the services provided by the provider.
     *
     * @return array
     */
    public function provides()
    {
      return array('vimeolist');
    }
}
```

5. Open the `app.php` file in the `app/config` directory, and in the `providers` array, add our service provider as follows:

```
'Matula\Vimeolist\VimeolistServiceProvider',
```

6. In the command line, run the following command:

php composer.phar dump-autoload

7. In `routes.php`, add a route to display the data as follows:

```
Route::get('vimeo/{username?}', function($username = null) use
($app)
{
  $vimeo = $app['vimeolist'];
  if ($username) {
      $vimeo->setUser($username);
  }
  dd($vimeo->getList());
});
```

How it works...

Our first step is to update our workbench's configuration file to hold our name and e-mail address. This will then be used for any other packages that we create in Laravel.

Next, we run the artisan command to create the files we need for our package. By using the `--resources` flag, it will also generate other files and directories that can be used specifically for Laravel. Once it's completed, there will be a new folder in our workbench directory that holds all our package's files. After drilling down into the directories, we'll get to a directory that holds our service provider file, and in this directory, we'll add our class file.

This example class will simply get a list of videos for a user from the Vimeo API. We have methods that will allow us to set a username, get the contents of the API endpoint, turn the JSON into a PHP object, and then create and return a formatted array. As a best practice, we should also make sure our code is tested and that we can put those files in the `test` directory.

To better integrate with Laravel, we need to update the service provider. We first update the `register` method and set the name we want to pass to Laravel's `app` variable and then we update the `provides` method to return the package name. Next, we need to update our app configuration file to actually register the service provider. Then, once we run the `dump-autoload` command in Composer, our new package will be available to use.

Finally, we create a route to interact with the package. We'll have one optional parameter, that is, the username. We also need to make sure the `$app` variable is available in our route. Then, when we call `$app['vimeolist']`, the service provider will automatically instantiate our class and allow us to access the Vimeo list. For our purposes, we're only using the `dd()` helper function of Laravel to display the data, but we could also pass it to a view and make it look nicer.

There's more...

Laravel also has the option to create a facade for our package, so we could call it using something similar to `$vimeo = Vimeolist::setUser()`. There are also many other options for packages that can be found in the documentation at `http://laravel.com/docs/packages`.

Adding your Composer package to Packagist

To make it easier to distribute our packages, we should submit them to the website `packagist.org`. In this recipe, we'll see how to set up our package on GitHub and add it to Packagist.

Getting ready

For this recipe, we'll need to have completed the *Creating a Composer package in Laravel* recipe, and we'll also need an active GitHub account.

How to do it...

To complete this recipe, follow these steps:

1. In the command line, move to the `workbench/matula/vimeolist` directory and set up our `git` repository as follows:

   ```
   git init
   git add -A
   git commit -m 'First Package commit'
   ```

2. Create a new GitHub repository at `https://github.com/new` and give it the name `vimeolist`.

3. Add our package to GitHub:

   ```
   git remote add origin git@github.com:{username}/vimeolist.git
   git push -u origin master
   ```

4. Go to `https://packagist.org/login/` and log in using your GitHub account.

5. Click on the green **Submit Package** button shown in the following screenshot:

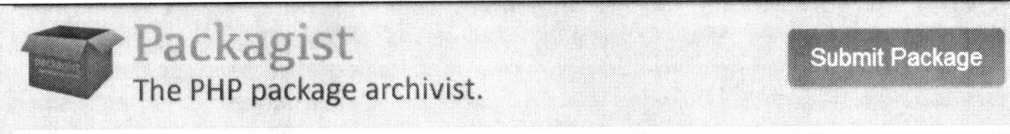

Packagist
The PHP package archivist.

Submit Package

6. In the **Repository URL** text field, add the Git read-only URL from GitHub as shown in the following screenshot:

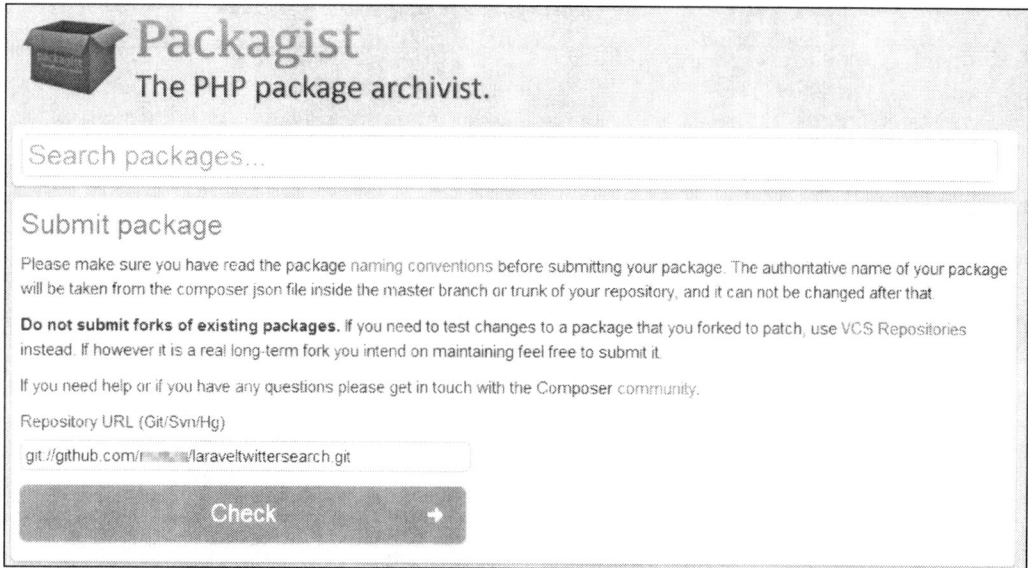

7. Click on **Check,** and if everything works, click on **Submit**.

How it works...

We begin by creating a `git` repository in our package's main directory. We then create a repository in GitHub for our files, add that remote to our local repository, and then push our local repository to GitHub.

On the Packagist site, we log in using our GitHub account and allow the `packagist.org` access. Then, we submit our packages at `https://packagist.org/packages/submit` using the GitHub URL from our repository. After clicking on **Check**, Packagist will look through the code and format it for use with Composer. If there are any errors, we will be prompted with what we need to do to fix them.

If everything checks out and we click on **Submit**, our package will then be listed on the Packagist website.

See also

▶   The *Creating a Composer package in Laravel* recipe

Adding a non-Packagist package to Composer

Adding a single line to our `composer.json` file and having Composer automatically download and install a package is great, but it requires the package to be available on `packagist.org`. In this recipe, we'll see how to install packages that aren't available on Packagist.

Getting ready

For this recipe, we'll need a standard Laravel installation.

How to do it...

To complete this recipe, follow these steps:

1. On GitHub, we'll need to find a package we want to use. For this example, we'll use the `UniversalForms` package found at `https://github.com/wesleytodd/Universal-Forms-PHP`.

2. Open our main `composer.json` file and update the `require` section as follows:

   ```
   "require": {
           "laravel/framework": "4.0.*",
           "wesleytodd/universal-forms": "dev-master"
       },
   ```

3. In `composer.json`, under the `require` section, add the repository we want to use:

   ```
   "repositories": [
           {
               "type": "vcs",
               "url": "https://github.com/wesleytodd/Universal-Forms-
   PHP"
           }
       ],
   ```

4. In the command line, update Composer as follows:

   `php composer.phar update`

5. Open the `app/config/app.php` file and update the `providers` array with the following line:

   ```
   'Wesleytodd\UniversalForms\Drivers\Laravel\
   UniversalFormsServiceProvider',
   ```

6. In `routes.php`, instantiate the class and use it on our routes as follows:

```
$form_json = '{
        "action" : "uform",
        "method" : "POST",
        "fields" : [
            {
                "name" : "name",
                "type" : "text",
                "label" : "Name",
                "rules" : ["required"]
            },
            {
                "name" : "email",
                "type" : "email",
                "label" : "Email",
                "value" : "myemail@example.com",
                "rules" : ["required", "email"]
            },
            {
                "name" : "message",
                "type" : "textarea",
                "label" : "Message",
                "rules" : ["required", "length[30,0]"]
            }
        ]
}';

$uform = new Wesleytodd\UniversalForms\Drivers\Laravel\Form($form_json);

Route::get('uform', function() use ($uform)
{
  return $uform->render();
});

Route::post('uform', function() use ($uform)
{
  // validate
  $valid = $uform->valid(Input::all());
  if ($valid) {
      // Could also save to database
      dd(Input::all());
  } else {
      // Could redirect back to form
      dd($uform->getErrors());
  }
});
```

How it works...

Our first step is to add in the line for the required packages just like with other Composer packages. However, since this package isn't available on `packagist.org`, it will throw an error if we try to update Composer. To get it to work, we need to add in a repository for Composer to use. Composer has many different options for using other repositories, and they can be found at `http://getcomposer.org/doc/05-repositories.md#vcs`.

Next, we update Composer and it will install the package for us. Since this package comes with a Laravel service provider, we then update our configuration file to register it.

Now we're able to use the package in our app. For our purposes, we'll instantiate the class outside of the routes and pass it into the routes' closure. Then we can use the library like normal. This particular package will take a JSON string or file and automatically create our form output for us.

Creating a custom artisan command

Laravel's artisan command-line tool makes many tasks easy to accomplish. If we want to make our own tasks and use artisan to run them, the process is quite simple. In this recipe, we'll see how to make an artisan task that automatically creates an HTML5 skeleton in our `views` directory.

Getting ready

For this recipe, we'll need a standard Laravel installation.

How to do it...

To complete this recipe, follow these steps:

1. In the command line, run the `artisan` command to create our needed files:

   php artisan command:make SkeletonCommand

2. In the `app/commands` directory, open the `SkeletonCommand.php` file and update the code as follows:

```php
<?php

use Illuminate\Console\Command;
use Symfony\Component\Console\Input\InputOption;
use Symfony\Component\Console\Input\InputArgument;
use Illuminate\Filesystem\Filesystem as File;

class SkeletonCommand extends Command {
```

```php
/**
 * The console command name.
 *
 * @var string
 */
protected $name = 'skeleton:make';

/**
 * The console command description.
 *
 * @var string
 */
protected $description = 'Creates an HTML5 skeleton
 view.';

 /**
    * File system instance
    *
    * @var File
    */
   protected $file;

/**
 * Create a new command instance.
 *
 * @return void
 */
public function __construct()
{
  parent::__construct();
  $this->file = new File();
}

/**
 * Execute the console command.
 *
 * @return void
 */
public function fire()
{
      $view = $this->argument('view');
      $file_name = 'app/views/' . $view;
      $ext = ($this->option('blade')) ? '.blade.php' :
      '.php';
          $template = '<!DOCTYPE html>
          <html>
          <head>
```

```
                    <meta charset=utf-8 />
                    <title></title>
                    <link rel="stylesheet" type="text/css"
                     media="screen" href="css/style.css" />
                     <script type="text/javascript"
                      src="http://ajax.googleapis.com/
                      ajax/libs/jquery/2.0.3/jquery.min.js">
                     </script>
                       <!--[if IE]>
                             <script src="http://html5shiv.
                             googlecode.com/svn/trunk
                             /html5.js"></script>
                       <![endif]-->
                </head>
                <body>
                </body>
                </html>';

                if (!$this->file->exists($file_name)) {
                    $this->info('HTML5 skeleton created!');
                    return $this->file->put($file_name . $ext,
                     $template) !== false;
            } else {
                    $this->info('HTML5 skeleton created!');
                    return $this->file->put($file_name . '-' .
                     time() . $ext, $template) !== false;
            }

        $this->error('There was a problem creating your
                    HTML5 skeleton');
            return false;
    }

/**
 * Get the console command arguments.
 *
 * @return array
 */
protected function getArguments()
{
    return array(
        array('view', InputArgument::REQUIRED,
            'The name of the view.'),
    );
}
```

```
/**
 * Get the console command options.
 *
 * @return array
 */
protected function getOptions()
{
    return array(
    array('blade', null, InputOption::VALUE_OPTIONAL,
            'Use Blade templating?', false),
    );
}

}
```

3. In the app/start directory, open the artisan.php file and add the following line:

   ```
   Artisan::add(new SkeletonCommand);
   ```

4. In the command line, test out the new command:

   php artisan skeleton:make MyNewView --blade=true

How it works...

Our first step is to use the command:make function of artisan and pass in the name of the command we want to use. After this runs, we'll find a new file in our app/commands directory with the same name as the name we chose.

In our SkeletonCommand file, we start by adding in a name. This will be the command to which artisan will respond. Next, we set a description, which will display when we list out all the artisan commands.

For this command, we'll be accessing the filesystem, so we need to make sure to add Laravel's Filesystem class and that we instantiate it in our constructor. Then, we come to the fire() method. This is where all the code we want to run should go. For our purpose, we use a single argument to determine what our view file name will be, and if the --blade parameter is set to true, we'll make it a blade file. Then, we create a string that holds our HTML5 skeleton, though we could also make this a separate file and pull in the text.

We then create the new file using the template as our HTML and display a success message in the console.

8
Using Ajax and jQuery

In this chapter, we will cover:

- ▶ Getting data from another page
- ▶ Setting up a controller to return JSON data
- ▶ Creating an Ajax search function
- ▶ Creating and validating a user using Ajax
- ▶ Filtering data based on checkbox selection
- ▶ Making an Ajax newsletter sign-up box
- ▶ Sending an e-mail using Laravel and jQuery
- ▶ Creating a sortable table using jQuery and Laravel

Introduction

Many modern web applications rely on JavaScript to add dynamic user interactions. Using the jQuery library and Laravel's built-in functions, we can create these interactions with ease in our own application.

We'll begin by receiving data asynchronously from other pages and proceed to send data that can be saved in a database.

Getting data from another page

In our application, there may be times when we need to access some HTML from another page. Using Laravel and jQuery, we can accomplish this easily.

Getting ready

For this recipe, we just need a standard Laravel installation.

How to do it...

To complete this recipe, follow the given steps:

1. Open the `routes.php` file:

```php
Route::get('getting-data', function()
{
    return View::make('getting-data');
});

Route::get('tab1', function()
{
    if (Request::ajax()) {
    return View::make('tab1');
}
    return Response::error('404');
});

Route::get('tab2', function()
{
    if (Request::ajax()) {
    return View::make('tab2');
}
    return Response::error('404');
});
```

2. In the `views` directory, create a file named `tab1.php`:

```html
<h1>CHAPTER 1 - Down the Rabbit-Hole</h1>
<p>
    Alice was beginning to get very tired of sitting by her
        sister on the bank,
    and of having nothing to do: once or twice she had peeped
        into the book her sister
    was reading, but it had no pictures or conversations in
        it, 'and what is the
    use of a book,' thought Alice 'without pictures or
        conversation?'
```

```
</p>
<p>
   So she was considering in her own mind (as well as she
      could, for the
   hot day made her feel very sleepy and stupid), whether
      the pleasure of making
   a daisy-chain would be worth the trouble of getting up
      and picking the daisies,
   when suddenly a White Rabbit with pink eyes ran close by
      her.
</p>
```

3. In the `views` directory, create a file named `tab2.php`:

```
<h1>Chapter 1</h1>
<p>"TOM!"</p>
<p>No answer.</p>
<p>"TOM!"</p>
<p>No answer.</p>
<p>"What's gone with that boy,  I wonder? You TOM!"</p>
<p>No answer.</p>
<p>
   The old lady pulled her spectacles down and looked over them
      about the room;
   then she put them up and looked out under them. She seldom
      or never looked
   through them for so small a thing as a boy; they were her
      state pair,
   the pride of her heart, and were built for "style," not
      service—she could
   have seen through a pair of stove-lids just as well. She
      looked perplexed
   for a moment, and then said, not fiercely, but still loud
      enough for the
   furniture to hear:
</p>
<p>"Well, I lay if I get hold of you I'll—"</p>
<p>
   She did not finish, for by this time she was bending down
      and punching
   under the bed with the broom, and so she needed breath to
      punctuate
   the punches with. She resurrected nothing but the cat.
</p>
```

4. In the `views` directory, create a file named `getting-data.php`:

```
<!DOCTYPE html>
<html>
<head>
  <meta charset=utf-8 />
  <title>Getting Data</title>
  <script type="text/javascript"
    src="//ajax.googleapis.com/ajax/libs/jquery
    /1.9.0/jquery.min.js"></script>
</head>
<body>
<ul>
  <li><a href="#" id="tab1" class="tabs">Alice In
    Wonderland</a></li>
  <li><a href="#" id="tab2" class="tabs">Tom Sawyer</a></li>
</ul>
<h1 id="title"></h1>
<div id="container"></div>
<script>
  $(function() {
  $(".tabs").on("click", function(e) {
    e.preventDefault();
  var tab = $(this).attr("id");
  var title = $(this).html();
  $("#container").html("loading...");
  $.get(tab, function(data) {
  $("#title").html(title);
  $("#container").html(data);
});
});
});
</script>
</body>
</html>
```

5. View the page at `http://{yourserver}/getting-data` and click on the links to load the content.

How it works...

We start by setting up our routes. Our first route is going to display links, and when we click on them, content will be loaded into the page. Our next two routes will hold the actual content to display on the main page. To make sure that these pages can't be accessed directly, we use the `Request::ajax()` method to make sure that only Ajax requests are accepted. If someone tries to access the page directly, it will send them to an error page.

Our two view files will hold a couple of excerpts from books. Since this will be loaded into another page, we don't need the full HTML. Our main page, however, is a full HTML page. We begin by loading jQuery using the **Content Delivery Network** (**CDN**) from Google. Then, we have a list of the books we want to use. To make things a little easier, the ID of the link will correspond to the routes we created.

When someone clicks on the link, the script will use the ID and get the content from the route with the same name. The results will be loaded into our `container` div.

Setting up a controller to return JSON data

When we access data using JavaScript, one of the easiest ways is to use JSON-formatted data. In Laravel, we can return JSON from one of our controllers to be used by our JavaScript on another page.

Getting ready

For this recipe, we need a standard Laravel installation.

How to do it...

For this recipe, follow the given steps:

1. In the `controllers` directory, create a file named `BooksController.php`:

```php
<?php

class BooksController extends BaseController {

public function getIndex()
{
return View::make('books.index');
}

public function getBooks()
{
$books = array(
  'Alice in Wonderland',
  'Tom Sawyer',
  'Gulliver\'s Travels',
  'Dracula',
  'Leaves of Grass'
  );
return Response::json($books);
}
}
```

2. In `routes.php`, register the books controller

```
Route::controller('books', 'BooksController');
```

3. In the `views` directory, create a folder named `books`, and in that folder, create a file named `index.php`:

```
<!DOCTYPE html>
<html>
<head>
  <meta charset=utf-8 />
  <title>Show Books</title>
  <script type="text/javascript"
    src="//ajax.googleapis.com/ajax/libs/jquery/1.9.0/
    jquery.min.js"></script>
</head>
<body>
<a href="#" id="book-button">Load Books</a>
<div id="book-list"></div>
<script>
$(function() {
$('#book-button').on('click', function(e) {
  e.preventDefault();
$('#book-list').html('loading...');
$.get('books/books', function(data) {
  var book_list = '';
$.each(data, function(){
  book_list += this + '<br>';
})
$("#book-list").html(book_list);
$('#book-button').hide();
});
});
});
</script>
</body>
</html>
```

How it works...

We begin by creating a RESTful controller for our book list which extends our `BaseController` class. Our controller has two methods: one to display the list and one to return the formatted list. Our `getBooks()` method uses an array as our data source, and we use Laravel's `Response::json()` method to automatically do the correct formatting for us.

On our main page, we do a `get` request to the page in JavaScript, receive the JSON, and loop through the results. As we loop, we add the books to a JavaScript variable and then add the list to our `book-list` div.

There's more...

Our list could come from any data source. We could add in database functionality or even call an API. When we use the JSON response from Laravel, that value is correctly formatted with the correct headers.

Creating an Ajax search function

If we want to search for information in our application, it might be useful to perform the search asynchronously. That way, the user won't have to be taken to a new page and have all the assets refreshed. Using Laravel and JavaScript, we can perform this search in a very simple manner.

Getting ready

For this recipe, we'll need a working installation of Laravel.

How to do it...

To complete this recipe, follow these steps:

1. In the `controllers` directory, create a file named `SearchController.php`:

```php
<?php

class SearchController extends BaseController {

  public function getIndex()
  {
    return View::make('search.index');
  }

  public function postSearch()
  {
    $return = array();
```

```
$term = Input::get('term');

$books = array(
   array('name' => 'Alice in Wonderland', 'author' => 'Lewis
Carroll'),
   array('name' => 'Tom Sawyer', 'author' => 'Mark
     Twain'),
   array('name' => 'Gulliver\'s Travels', 'author' =>
     'Jonathan Swift'),
   array('name' => 'The Art of War', 'author' => 'Sunzi'),
   array('name' => 'Dracula', 'author' => 'Bram Stoker'),
   array('name' => 'War and Peace', 'author' =>
     'LeoTolstoy'),
   );

foreach ($books as $book) {
if (stripos($book['name'], $term) !== FALSE) $return[] =
   $book;
}

return Response::json($return);
}
}
```

2. In the `routes.php` file, register the controller:

```
Route::controller('search', 'SearchController');
```

3. In the `views` directory, create a folder named `search`, and in that folder, create a file named `index.php`:

```
<!DOCTYPE html>
<html>
<head>
<meta charset=utf-8 />
<title>AJAX Search</title>
<script type="text/javascript"
  src="//ajax.googleapis.com/ajax/libs/jquery/
    1.9.0/jquery.min.js"></script>
</head>
<body>
<h1>Search</h1>
<form id="search-form">
<input name="search" id="term"> <input type="submit">
</form>
<div id="results"></div>
<script>
  $(function() {
  $("#search-form").on("submit", function(e) {
    e.preventDefault();
```

```
    var search_term = $("#term").val();
    var display_results = $("#results");
    display_results.html("loading...");
    var results = '';
    $.post("search/search", {term: search_term}, function(data)
        {
        if (data.length == 0) {
        results = 'No Results';
    } else {
    $.each(data, function() {
    results += this.name + ' by ' + this.author + '<br>';
});
}
display_results.html(results);
});
})
});
</script>
</body>
</html>
```

How it works...

We first create a RESTful controller that holds two methods: one for our main page and one to process the search. On our main page, we have a single `text` field and a `submit` button. When the form is submitted, our JavaScript will post the form to our search page. If there are results, it will loop through them and display them in our `results` div.

For our `postSearch()` method, we use an array as our data source. When a search is posted, we then loop through the array to see if the string matches any of our titles. If so, the value is added to an array and that array is returned as a JSON.

Creating and validating a user using Ajax

When a user comes to our application, we may want them to register or login without the need to navigate to another page. Using Ajax within Laravel, we can submit the user's form and run the validation asynchronously.

Getting ready

For this recipe, we'll need a working installation of Laravel as well as a properly configured MySQL database. We also need to add a user table to our database, which we can do with the following code:

```
CREATE TABLE users (
    id int(10) unsigned NOT NULL AUTO_INCREMENT,
    email varchar(255) DEFAULT NULL,
    password char(60) DEFAULT NULL,
    PRIMARY KEY (id)
    ) ENGINE=InnoDB DEFAULT CHARSET=utf8;
```

How to do it...

To complete this recipe, follow the given steps:

1. In the `controllers` directory, create a `UsersController.php` file:

```php
<?php
class UsersController extends BaseController {
  public function getIndex()
  {
  return View::make('users.index');
  }

  public function postRegister()
  {
  $rules = array(
    'email' => 'required|email',
    'password' => 'required|min:6'
    );

  $validation = Validator::make(Input::all(), $rules);

  if ($validation->fails())
  {
  return Response::json($validation->errors()->toArray());
  }
  else
  {
  DB::table('users')->insert(array(
    'email' => Input::get('email'),
    'password' => Hash::make(Input::get('password'))
    ));
  return Response::json(array('Registration is complete!'));
  }
  }
  }
```

2. Register the controller in `routes.php`:

```
Route::controller('users', 'UsersController');
```

3. In the `views` directory, create a folder named `users`, and in that folder, create a file named `index.php`:

```
<!doctype html>
<html lang="en">
  <head>
  <meta charset="utf-8">
  <title>User Register</title>
  <script type="text/javascript"
    src="http://ajax.googleapis.com/ajax/libs/jquery/
    1.9.0/jquery.min.js"></script>
  </head>
  <body>
  <form id="register">
  <label for="email">Your email:</label>
  <input type="email" name="email" id="email"><br>
  <label for="password">Your password:</label>
  <input type="password" name="password" id="password"><br>
  <input type="submit">
  </form>
  <div id="results"></div>
  <script>
  $(function(){
  $("#register").on("submit", function(e) {
    e.preventDefault();
  var results = '';
  $.post('users/register',
    {email: $("#email").val(), password:
    $("#password").val()}, function(data) {
  $.each(data, function(){
    results += this + '<br>';
});
  $("#results").html(results);
});
});
});
</script>
  </body>
</html>
```

How it works...

To begin this recipe, we create our main page which will hold our user registration form. When the form is submitted, it will post to our `postRegister()` method and return any results to the `results` div.

The `postRegister()` method begins by setting up the rules for our validation. In this case, we want to make sure both fields have a value, the e-mail must be valid, and the password must be at least 6 characters. If the validation fails, we send the error back as a JSON-encoded string and our main page will display the error. If everything is valid, we then save everything to the database and return a success message.

There's more...

If we don't want any other pages to post data to our method, we could add a `Request::ajax()` conditional. This would mean that only Ajax calls would be processed by our method.

Filtering data based on checkbox selection

When displaying data to a user, it could be convenient to allow them to filter the data. So we don't have to make the user click on submit and reload the page every time, we can do all the filtering using Ajax. For this recipe, we'll make a book list and allow the user to filter it based on the genre.

Getting ready

For this recipe, we need a standard Laravel installation that's configured to work with a database. We'll need to set up a table to use by running this SQL statement:

```
DROP TABLE IF EXISTS books;
CREATE TABLE books (
  id int(10) unsigned NOT NULL AUTO_INCREMENT,
  name varchar(255) DEFAULT NULL,
  author varchar(255) DEFAULT NULL,
  genre varchar(255) DEFAULT NULL,
  PRIMARY KEY (id)
) ENGINE=InnoDB DEFAULT CHARSET=latin1;

INSERT INTO books VALUES ('1', 'Alice in Wonderland',
  'Lewis Carroll', 'fantasy');
INSERT INTO books VALUES ('2', 'Tom Sawyer', 'Mark
  Twain', 'comedy');
INSERT INTO books VALUES ('3', 'Gulliver\'s Travels',
  'Jonathan Swift', 'fantasy');
```

```
INSERT INTO books VALUES ('4', 'The Art of War', 'Sunzi',
    'philosophy');
INSERT INTO books VALUES ('5', 'Dracula', 'Bram Stoker',
    'horror');
INSERT INTO books VALUES ('6', 'War and Peace', 'Leo
    Tolstoy', 'drama');
INSERT INTO books VALUES ('7', 'Frankenstein', 'Mary
    Shelley', 'horror');
INSERT INTO books VALUES ('8', 'The Importance of Being
    Earnest', 'Oscar Wilde', 'comedy');
INSERT INTO books VALUES ('9', 'Peter Pan', 'J. M.
    Barrie', 'fantasy');
```

How to do it...

To complete this recipe, follow these steps:

1. In the `controllers` directory, create a new file named `BooksController.php`:

```php
<?php
class BooksController extends BaseController {
  public function getIndex()
{
  return View::make('books.index');
}

  public function postBooks()
{
  if (!$genre = Input::get('genre')) {
  $books = Book::all();
  } else {
  $books = Book::whereIn('genre', $genre)->get();
}
return $books;
}
}
```

2. Register the `books` controller in the `routes.php` file:

```
Route::controller('books', 'BooksController');
```

3. In the `views` directory, create a new folder named `books`, and in that folder, create a file named `index.php`:

```
<!doctype html>
<html lang="en">
  <head>
  <meta charset="utf-8">
```

```html
<title>Books filter</title>
<scriptsrc="//ajax.googleapis.com/ajax/libs/jquery
    /1.10.2/jquery.min.js"></script>
</head>
<body>
<form id="filter">
Comedy: <input type="checkbox" name="genre[]"
    value="comedy"><br>
Drama: <input type="checkbox" name="genre[]"
    value="drama"><br>
Fantasy: <input type="checkbox" name="genre[]"
    value="fantasy"><br>
Horror: <input type="checkbox" name="genre[]"
    value="horror"><br>
Philosophy: <input type="checkbox" name="genre[]"
    value="philosophy"><br>
</form>
<hr>
<h3>Results</h3>
<div id="books"></div>
<script>
$(function(){
$("input[type=checkbox]").on('click', function() {
    var books = '';
$("#books").html('loading...');
$.post('books/books', $("#filter").serialize(),
    function(data){
    $.each(data, function(){
    books += this.name + ' by ' + this.author + ' (' +
    this.genre + ')<br>';
});
$("#books").html(books);
});
});
});
</script>
</body>
</html>
```

4. In the `models` directory, create a file named `Book.php`:

```php
<?php
class Book extends Eloquent {
}
```

5. In the browser, go to `http://{my-server}/books` and click on a few checkboxes to see the result.

How it works...

With our database set up, we begin with our main list page. This page has a number of checkboxes, with the value of each corresponding to a genre in our books table. When a box is checked, the form is submitted asynchronously to our `postBooks()` method. We use those results, loop through them, and display them in our `books` div.

Our `postBooks()` method begins by making sure a genre was actually submitted. If not, that means everything is unchecked and it will return all the books. If something is checked, we get everything from the database that matches the checked values. Since Laravel provides us with the raw returned data in JSON format, we then return the results, and in our index, the results are displayed correctly.

Making an Ajax newsletter sign-up box

One way to have users added to our e-mail list is to have them sign-up through our website. In this recipe, we'll be using MailChimp's API and a modal window to show a sign-up form and have it sent through an Ajax call.

Getting ready

For this recipe, we'll need a standard Laravel installation. We'll also be using the MailChimp API for the newsletter; a free account and API key can be created at `www.mailchimp.com`.

How to do it...

To complete this recipe, follow the given steps:

1. Open the `composer.json` file and update the `require` section to resemble the following code:

   ```
   "require": {
   "laravel/framework": "4.0.*",
   "rezzza/mailchimp": "dev-master"
   }
   ```

2. In the command-line window, where the artisan file is located, update Composer with the following command:

   ```
   php composer.phar update
   ```

3. In the `app/config` directory, create a file named `mailchimp.php`:

```php
<?php

return array(
  'key' => '12345abcde-us1',
  'list' => '123456789'
);
```

4. In the `views` directory, create a file named `signup.php`:

```html
<!doctype html>
<html lang="en">
  <head>
  <meta charset="utf-8">
  <title>Newsletter Signup</title>
  <link href="//netdna.bootstrapcdn.com/twitter-
    bootstrap/2.2.2/css/bootstrap-combined.min.css"
    rel="stylesheet">
  <script src="//ajax.googleapis.com/ajax/libs/jquery/
    1.9.0/jquery.min.js"></script>
  <script src="//netdna.bootstrapcdn.com/twitter-
    bootstrap/2.2.2/js/bootstrap.min.js"></script>
  </head>
  <body>
  <p>
  <a href="#signupModal" role="button" class="btn btn-info"
    data-toggle="modal">Newsletter Signup</a>
  </p>
  <div id="results"></div>
  <div id="signupModal" class="modal hide fade">
  <div class="modal-header">
  <button type="button" class="close" data-dismiss="modal"
    aria-hidden="true">&times;</button>
  <h3>Sign-up for our awesome newsletter!</h3>
  </div>
  <div class="modal-body">
  <p>
  <form id="newsletter_form">
  <label>Your First Name</label>
  <input name="fname"><br>
  <label>Last Name</label>
  <input name="lname"><br>
  <label>Email</label>
  <input name="email">
  </form>
  </p>
  </div>
  <div class="modal-footer">
```

```
<a href="#" class="btn close" data-
  dismiss="modal">Close</a>
<a href="#" class="btn btn-primary"
  id="newsletter_submit">Signup</a>
</div>
</div>
<script>
$(function(){
$("#newsletter_submit").on('click', function(e){
  e.preventDefault();
$("#results").html("loading...");
$.post('signup-submit',
  $("#newsletter_form").serialize(),
  function(data){
$('#signupModal').modal('hide');
$("#results").html(data);
});
});
});
</script>
</body>
</html>
```

5. In the `routes.php` file, add the routes we need with the following code:

```php
Route::get('signup', function()
{
  return View::make('signup');
});

Route::post('signup-submit', function()
{
  $mc = new MCAPI(Config::get('mailchimp.key'));

  $response = $mc->listSubscribe(
    '{list_id}',
    Input::get('email'),
    array(
    'FNAME' => Input::get('fname'),
    'LNAME' => Input::get('lname')
)
);

if ($mc->errorCode){
return 'There was an error: ' . $mc->errorMessage;
} else {
return 'You have been subscribed!';
}
});
```

How it works...

We start by installing the MailChimp package into our application using a composer version of the MailChimp SDK. We then need to create a configuration file to hold our API key and the list ID we want to use.

Our sign-up page will utilize jQuery and Bootstrap for our processing and display. Since we only want to display the form when the user wants to sign-up, we have a single button that, when clicked on, will display a modal window with our form. The form will take out first name, last name, and e-mail address.

When the sign-up form is submitted, we serialize the data and send it to our `signup-submit` route. Once we get a response, we hide the modal and display the results on our page.

In our `signup-submit` route, we attempt to subscribe the user with the information entered. If we get a response, we check if the response includes an error. If there is an error, we display that to the user, and if not, we show our success message.

There's more...

Our `signup-submit` route isn't doing any validation on the form input. To include that, look at the an example in the *Creating and validating a user using Ajax* recipe.

See also

▸   The *Creating and validating a user using Ajax* recipe

Sending an e-mail using Laravel and jQuery

When creating a contact form, we may choose to let the user send the form asynchronously. Using Laravel and jQuery, we can have the form submitted without needing the user to go to a different page.

Getting ready

For this recipe, we need a standard Laravel installation and our mail client properly configured. We can update our mail configuration in the `app/config/mail.php` file.

How to do it...

To complete this recipe, follow the given steps:

1. In the `views` directory, create a file named `emailform.php` as shown in the following code:

```html
<!doctype html>
<html lang="en">
<head>
<meta charset="utf-8">
<title></title>
<script src="//ajax.googleapis.com/ajax/libs
  /jquery/1.10.2/jquery.min.js"></script>
</head>
<body>
<div id="container">
<div id="error"></div>
<form id="email-form">
<label>To: </label>
<input name="to" type="email"><br>
<label>From: </label>
<input name="from" type="email"><br>
<label>Subject: </label>
<input name="subject"><br>
<label>Message:</label><br>
<textarea name="message"></textarea><br>
<input type="submit" value="Send">
</form>
</div>
<script>
$(function(){
$("#email-form").on('submit', function(e){
  e.preventDefault();
$.post('email-send', $(this).serialize(), function(data){
if (data == 0) {
$("#error").html('<h3>There was an error</h3>');
} else {
if (isNaN(data)) {
$("#error").html('<h3>' + data + '</h3>');
} else {
$("#container").html('Your email has been sent!');
}
}
});
});
});
</script>
</body>
</html>
```

2. In the `views` folder, create our e-mail template view file named `ajaxemail.php` with the following code:

```php
<!DOCTYPE html>
<html lang="en-US">
<head>
<meta charset="utf-8">
</head>
<body>
<h2>Your Message:</h2>
<div><?= $message ?></div>
</body>
</html>
```

3. In the `routes.php` file, create the routes as given in the following code snippet:

```php
Route::get('email-form', function()
{
  return View::make('emailform');
});
  Route::post('email-send', function()
{
  $input = Input::all();

  $rules = array(
    'to'      => 'required|email',
    'from'    => 'required|email',
    'subject' => 'required',
    'message' => 'required'
);

  $validation = Validator::make($input, $rules);

  if ($validation->fails())
{
  $return = '';
  foreach ($validation->errors()->all() as $err) {
  $return .= $err . '<br>';
}
  return $return;
}

  $send = Mail::send('ajaxemail', array('message' =>
    Input::get('message')), function($message)
{
  $message->to(Input::get('to'))
    ->replyTo(Input::get('from'))
    ->subject(Input::get('subject'));
});

  return $send;
});
```

How it works...

For this recipe, we need to have our e-mail client properly configured. We have many options to choose from, including PHP's `mail()` method, sendmail, and SMTP. We could even use a third-party e-mail service such as mailgun or postmark.

Our e-mail form is a regular HTML form with four fields: the `to` and `from` e-mail addresses, the `subject` line, and the actual e-mail message. When the form is submitted, the fields are serialized and posted to our `email-send` route.

The `email-send` route first validates all of the posted input. If there are any validation errors, they are returned back as a string. If everything checks out, we send our values to the `Mail::send` method and then send it.

Back in our `e-mail-form` route JavaScript, we check if `email-send` returned `FALSE`, and if so, we display an error. If not, we need to check if the response was a number or not. If it wasn't a number, that means there were validation errors and we display them. If it is a number, that means the e-mail was sent successfully, so we display a success message.

Creating a sortable table using jQuery and Laravel

When handling large amounts of data, it can be helpful to display it in a table view. To manipulate the data, such as for sorting or searching, we can use the data tables JavaScript library. This way, we don't need to keep making database calls every time we want to change the view.

Getting ready

For this recipe, we need a standard installation of Laravel and a properly configured MySQL database.

How to do it...

Follow the given steps to complete this recipe:

1. In our database, create a new table and add some example data using the following commands:

```
DROP TABLE IF EXISTS bookprices;
CREATE TABLE bookprices (
    id int(10) unsigned NOT NULL AUTO_INCREMENT,
    price float(10,2) DEFAULT NULL,
    book varchar(100) DEFAULT NULL,
    PRIMARY KEY (id)
    ) ENGINE=InnoDB DEFAULT CHARSET=utf8;
```

```
INSERT INTO bookprices VALUES ('1', '14.99', 'Alice in
  Wonderland');
INSERT INTO bookprices VALUES ('2', '24.50',
  'Frankenstein');
INSERT INTO bookprices VALUES ('3', '29.80', 'War and
  Peace');
INSERT INTO bookprices VALUES ('4', '11.08', 'Moby
  Dick');
INSERT INTO bookprices VALUES ('5', '19.72', 'The Wizard
  of Oz');
INSERT INTO bookprices VALUES ('6', '45.00', 'The
  Odyssey');
```

2. In the `app/models` directory, create a file named `Bookprices.php` with the following code snippet:

```php
<?php
class Bookprices extends Eloquent {
}
```

3. In the `routes.php` file, add our route as given in the following code:

```php
Route::get('table', function()
{
   $bookprices = Bookprices::all();
   return View::make('table')->with('bookprices',
     $bookprices);
});
```

4. In the `views` directory, create a file named `table.php` with the following code:

```html
<!doctype html>
<html lang="en">
  <head>
  <meta charset="utf-8">
  <title></title>
  <script src="//ajax.googleapis.com/ajax/libs/jquery
    /1.10.2/jquery.min.js"></script>
  <script src="//ajax.aspnetcdn.com/ajax/jquery.dataTables
    /1.9.4/jquery.dataTables.min.js"></script>
  <link rel="stylesheet" type="text/css" href="
    //ajax.aspnetcdn.com/ajax/jquery.dataTables/
    1.9.4/css/jquery.dataTables.css">
  </head>
  <body>
  <h1>Book List</h1>
  <table>
  <thead>
  <tr>
```

```
<th>Price</th>
<th>Name</th>
</tr>
</thead>
<tbody>
<?php foreach ($bookprices as $book): ?>
<tr>
<td><?php echo $book['price'] ?></td>
<td><?php echo $book['book'] ?></td>
</tr>
<?php endforeach; ?>
</tbody>
</table>
<script>
$(function(){
$("table").dataTable();
});
</script>
</body>
</html>
```

How it works...

To start this recipe, we create a table to hold our book price data. We then insert the data into the table. Next, we create an `Eloquent` model so we can interact with the data. We then pass that data into our view.

In our view, we load in jQuery and the `dataTables` plugin. Then, we create a table to hold our data and then loop through the data, putting each record into a new row. When we add the `dataTable` plugin to our table, it will automatically add sorting to our table for each of our columns.

There's more...

`Datatables` is a powerful jQuery plugin to manipulate tabular data. For much more information, view the documentation at `http://www.datatables.net`.

9
Using Security and Sessions Effectively

In this chapter, we will cover:

- ▶ Encrypting and decrypting data
- ▶ Hashing passwords and other data
- ▶ Using CSRF tokens and filters in forms
- ▶ Using advanced validation in forms
- ▶ Building a shopping cart
- ▶ Using Redis to save sessions
- ▶ Using basic sessions and cookies
- ▶ Creating a secure API server

Introduction

Security is one of the most important things we need to consider when building web applications, especially if we're dealing with sensitive user information. Laravel provides many ways for us to keep our application secure.

In this chapter, we'll look at various ways to mask sensitive data, how to secure our forms from cross-site attacks, and how to secure an API. We'll also see how we can use sessions for building a shopping cart and using Redis to store session data.

Encrypting and decrypting data

When writing applications that deal with sensitive data, we may often want to encrypt any data that we store in our database. Laravel provides us with a solution to do just that.

Getting ready

For this recipe, we need a standard installation of Laravel, as well as a properly set-up and configured MySQL database.

How to do it...

This is how we'll complete the recipe using the following steps:

1. In the app/config directory, open the app.php file and make sure the key is empty

    ```
    'key' => '',
    ```

2. In the command line, go to the root of the application and generate a new key using the following command:

    ```
    php artisan key:generate
    ```

3. Create a table in the database to hold our sensitive information using this following command:

    ```
    CREATE TABLE accounts(
        id int(11) unsigned NOT NULL AUTO_INCREMENT,
        business varchar(255) DEFAULT NULL,
        total_revenue varchar(255) DEFAULT NULL,
        projected_revenue varchar(255) DEFAULT NULL,
        PRIMARY KEY (id))
        ENGINE=InnoDB DEFAULT CHARSET=utf8;
    ```

4. In our app/models directory, create a file named as Account.php by entering the following code:

    ```php
    <?php

    class Account extends Eloquent {
      protected $table = 'accounts';
      public $timestamps = false;
      public function setBusinessAttribute($business) {
        $this->attributes['business'] =
        Crypt::encrypt($business);
      }
    }
    ```

```php
public function setTotalrevenueAttribute($total_revenue)
  {$this->attributes['total_revenue'] =
    Crypt::encrypt($total_revenue);
}

  public function
    setProjectedrevenueAttribute($projected_revenue)
{
  $this->attributes['projected_revenue'] =
    Crypt::encrypt($projected_revenue);
}

public function getBusinessAttribute()
{
  return Crypt::decrypt($this->attributes['business'])
}

public function getTotalrevenueAttribute()
{
  return number_format(Crypt::decrypt($this
    >attributes['total_revenue'])) ;
}

public function getProjectedrevenueAttribute()
{
  return number_format(Crypt::decrypt($this
    >attributes['projected_revenue']));
}
}
```

5. In our `routes.php` file, create the routes to view and submit information by adding the following code:

```php
Route::get('accounts', function()
{
  $accounts = Account::all();
  return View::make('accounts')->with('accounts',
    $accounts);
});

Route::post('accounts', function()
{
  $account = new Account();
  $account->business = Input::get('business');
  $account->total_revenue = Input::get('total_revenue');
  $account->projected_revenue =
    Input::get('projected_revenue');
  $account->save();
  return Redirect::to('accounts');
});
```

6. In our `views` directory, create a file named as `accounts.php`

```
<form action="accounts" method="post">
<label for="business">Business:</label><br>
<input name="business"><br><br>
<label for="total_revenue">Total Revenue ($):</label><br>
<input name="total_revenue"><br><br>
<label for="projected_revenue">Projected Revenue
    ($):</label><br>
<input name="projected_revenue"><br><br>
<input type="submit">
</form>
<hr>
<?php if ($accounts): ?>
<table border="1">
<thead>
<tr>
<th>Business</th>
<th>Total Revenue</th>
<th>Projected Revenue</th>
</tr>
</thead>
<tbody>
<?php foreach ($accounts as $account): ?>
<tr>
<td><?= $account->business ?></td>
<td>$<?= $account->total_revenue ?></td>
<td>$<?= $account->projected_revenue ?></td>
</tr>
<?php endforeach; ?>
</tbody>
</table>
<?php endif; ?>
```

How it works...

We begin by removing the default key that comes with Laravel. Then, we use the `artisan` command to generate a new key for us and it's automatically saved in the correct file. The `artisan` command creates a fairly strong key, so we don't have to worry about coming up with one on our own.

After you have created a key for an application, make sure it doesn't get changed, as that will break your application if you've already used some encryption.

Then we set up a database table that will hold our sensitive data. In this example, we'll be storing business names along with some of their financial data.

Our next step is to set up our model, using the `Eloquent` model. To make things a little easier, we'll use the getters and setters in the model, so that whenever a value is set in our `Account` model, it will automatically get encrypted using the Laravel `Crypt::encrypt` class. Also, to get the information back out of the database, our model will automatically decrypt it for us.

Next, we create a couple of routes. The first route will show a form to add in information, as well as display anything already saved in the database. The next route simply takes the form input and saves it to a new row in our accounts table. After adding the information, we'll be redirected back to the account list and form page and the new data will be displayed at the bottom of the page.

However, if we look at the database itself, the information we're storing is unreadable text. This way, if someone happens to hack into our database, they won't get much information.

Hashing passwords and other data

It's common practice to hash a user's password when we store it in a database. This helps prevent anyone who gets unauthorized access to the database from seeing people's passwords. However, we may also want to hide our user's e-mail address or other information, so no one will be able to access them as well. We can use Laravel's **Hash** to do this easily.

Getting ready

For this recipe, we need a standard installation of Laravel, as well as a properly set-up and configured MySQL database.

How to do it...

Here are the steps for this recipe...

1. Set up the database table by using the following commands:

```
CREATE TABLE register (
    id int(10) unsigned NOT NULL AUTO_INCREMENT,
    username varchar(255) DEFAULT NULL,
    email char(60) DEFAULT NULL,
    password char(60) DEFAULT NULL,
    PRIMARY KEY (id)
    ) ENGINE=InnoDB AUTO_INCREMENT=1
```

2. In the `views` directory, create a file named as `register.php` with the help of the following code:

```php
<!doctype html>
<html lang="en">
<head>
<meta charset="utf-8">
<title>Register</title>
</head>
<body>
<p>
<h3>Register</h3>
<form method="post" action="register">
<label>User Name</label>
<input name="username"><br>
<label>Email</label>
<input name="email"><br>
<label>Password</label>
<input name="password"><br>
<input type="submit">
</form>
</p>
<p style="border-top:1px solid #555">
<h3>Login</h3>
<form method="post" action="login">
<label>User Name</label>
<input name="username"><br>
<label>Email</label>
<input name="email"><br>
<label>Password</label>
<input name="password"><br>
<input type="submit">
</form>
</p>
<hr>
<table border='1'>
<?php if ($users): ?>
<tr>
<th>User Name</th>
<th>Email</th>
<th>Password</th>
</tr>
<?php foreach ($users as $user): ?>
<tr>
<td><?= $user->username ?></td>
<td><?= $user->email ?></td>
<td><?= $user->password ?></td>
```

```
    </tr>
    <?php endforeach; ?>
    <?php endif; ?>
    </table>
    </body>
    </html>
```

3. In our `routes.php` file, create our routes by adding the following code:

```php
Route::get('register', function()
{
  $users = DB::table('register')->get();
  return View::make('register')->with('users', $users);
});


Route::post('register', function()
{
  $data = array(
    'username' => Input::get('username'),
    'email' => Hash::make(Input::get('email')),
    'password' => Hash::make(Input::get('password')));

  DB::table('register')->insert($data);

  return Redirect::to('register');
});


Route::post('login', function()
{
  $user = DB::table('register')->where('username', '=',
    Input::get('username'))->first();
  if (!is_null($user) and Hash::check(Input::get('email'),
    $user->email) and Hash::check(Input::get('password'),
    $user->password)) {
    echo "Log in successful";
  } else {
    echo "Not able to login";
  }
});
```

How it works...

To start this recipe, we first set up a basic users table to hold a username, e-mail address, and password. In this example, the username is the only thing that will need to be in regular text.

In our view, we'll create two forms—one for registering, and one for logging in. Just to show the raw data from the database, we'll also display a list of all the users, as well as the way their e-mail and password will look in the table.

When we submit the registration form, the information is posted to our register route and put into an array. For the e-mail and password, we use Laravel's `Hash::make()` function to hash it. We then insert the array into our register table and redirect back to the form and list page.

After redirecting, we'll see the new row added, our e-mail and password hashed, and an unrecognizable string. Interestingly, with the way hashing works, we could add two rows using the exact same data, and the hashes would be totally different.

Next, we can try to log in using the username, e-mail, and password. That route will grab a row from our table that corresponds with the username, then run Laravel's `Hash::check()` function on the input values and the database results. If it passes, it returns TRUE and we can proceed to our application.

There's more...

To use this recipe in a production environment, we'd need some validation on the input. We might also want to utilize the **Eloquent ORM** to make hashing a little easier.

If we don't need to hide our users' emails, we could also use Laravel's built in `Auth::attempt()` method. More information about that can be found on the Laravel website: `http://laravel.com/docs/security#authenticating-users`

Using CSRF tokens and filters in forms

Web forms are notorious for hackers trying to access a website or user's information. To make our forms a little more secure, we can use a **Cross-Site Request Forgery** (**CSRF**) strategy that's built into Laravel. This will stop form submissions from outside the user's session.

Getting ready

For this recipe, we need a standard installation of Laravel.

How to do it...

The following are the steps to complete this recipe:

1. In the `routes.php` file, create routes to hold and process the form by the code given below:

```
Route::get('cross-site', function()
{
  return View::make('cross-site');
});
```

```
Route::post('cross-site', array('before' => 'csrf',
  function()
{
  echo 'Token: ' . Session::token() . '<br>';
  dd(Input::all());
}));
```

2. In the `filters.php` file, make sure the `filter` for the `csrf` token is present as given in the following code:

```
Route::filter('csrf', function()
{
  if (Session::token() != Input::get('_token'))
{
  throw new Illuminate\Session\TokenMismatchException;
}
});
```

3. In our `views` directory, create a file named as `cross-site.php`, and add two forms for testing as given in the following code:

```
<!doctype html>
<html lang="en">
<head>
<meta charset="utf-8">
<title>CSRF Login</title>
</head>
<body>
<p>
<h3>CSRF Login</h3>
<?= Form::open(array('url' => 'cross-site', 'method' =>
  'post')) ?>
<?= Form::token() ?>
<?= Form::label('email', 'Email') ?>
<?= Form::text('email') ?>
<?= Form::label('password', 'Password') ?>
<?= Form::password('password') ?>
<?= Form::submit('Submit') ?>
<?= Form::close() ?>
</p>
<hr>
<p>
<h3>CSRF Fake Login</h3>
<?= Form::open(array('url' => 'cross-site', 'method' =>
  'post')) ?>
<?= Form::hidden('_token', 'smurftacular') ?>
<?= Form::label('email', 'Email') ?>
```

```
<?= Form::text('email') ?>
<?= Form::label('password', 'Password') ?>
<?= Form::password('password') ?>
<?= Form::submit('Submit') ?>
<?= Form::close() ?>
</p>
</body>
</html>
```

4. In the browser, go to `http://{your-server}/cross-site`
    (where `{your-server}` is the name of the server we're working on),
    and then submit each form to see the results.

How it works...

Our first step is to create the route for our CSRF form. In the form, all we need to do is add the `Form::token()` function; this will insert a hidden field with the name `_token`, and the value of our user session ID. For the route where the form is submitted, we add the `csrf` before filter to our route. If the request is determined to be forged, the page will return with a server error.

Our next form is an example of what would happen if a request was trying to be forged. For this form, instead of the `Form::token()` function, we manually add the hidden field and add some random value. Then when we submit the form, the page will display a fail message with a `TokenMismatchException` error.

There's more...

Laravel will also generate a `csrf` token automatically when you use the `Form::open()` function, so you don't need to add it manually.

Using advanced validation in forms

There might be times when we need to validate our forms for something that's not part of the framework. This recipe will show you how to build a custom validation rule and apply it.

Getting ready

For this recipe, we need a standard installation of Laravel.

How to do it...

The following are the steps to complete this recipe:

1. In the `views` directory, create a file named `valid.php` to hold our form using the following code:

```
<!doctype html>
<html lang="en">
<head>
<meta charset="utf-8">
<title>Custom Validation</title>
</head>
<body>
<p>
<?php if ($errors): ?>
<?php echo $errors->first('email') ?>
<?php echo $errors->first('captain') ?>
<?php endif; ?>
</p>
<p>
<h3>Custom Validation</h3>
<?= Form::open(array('url' => 'valid', 'method' => 'post'))
    ?>
<?= Form::label('email', 'Email') ?>
<?= Form::text('email') ?><br><br>
<?= Form::label('captain', 'Your favorite captains (choose
    three)') ?><br>
<?= 'Pike: ' . Form::checkbox('captain[]', 'Pike') ?><br>
<?= 'Kirk: ' . Form::checkbox('captain[]', 'Kirk') ?><br>
<?= 'Picard: ' . Form::checkbox('captain[]', 'Picard')
    ?><br>
<?= 'Sisko: ' . Form::checkbox('captain[]', 'Sisko') ?><br>
<?= 'Janeway: ' . Form::checkbox('captain[]', 'Janeway')
    ?><br>
<?= 'Archer: ' . Form::checkbox('captain[]', 'Archer')
    ?><br>
<?= 'Crunch: ' . Form::checkbox('captain[]', 'Crunch')
    ?><br>
<?= Form::submit('Submit') ?>
<?= Form::close() ?>
</p>
</body>
</html>
```

2. In the `routes.php` file, create our routes with the following code:

```
Route::get('valid', function()
{
  return View::make('valid');
});
Route::post('valid', function()
{
  $rules = array('email' => 'required|email',
    'captain' => 'required|check_three');
  $messages = array(
    'check_three' => 'Thou shalt choose three captains. No
    more. No less. Three shalt be the number thou shalt
    choose, and the number of the choosing shall be
    three.',);
  $validation = Validator::make(Input::all(), $rules,
    $messages);
  if ($validation->fails())
  {
  return Redirect::to('valid')->withErrors($validation);
  }
  echo "Form is valid!";
});
```

3. Also in the `routes.php` file, create our custom validation as given in the following code:

```
Validator::extend('check_three', function($attribute,
  $value, $parameters)
{
  return count($value) == 3;
});
```

How it works...

To begin, we create the form in our view. We ask for a valid e-mail and exactly three of the checkboxes to be checked. Since there's no Laravel validation method for exactly three checkboxes, we need to create a custom validation.

Our custom validation takes the input array and does a simple count. If it comes up to three, it returns TRUE. If not, it returns FALSE and fails the validation.

Back in our form processing route, all we then need to do is add the name of the custom validator we created to our validation rules. If we want to set a custom message, we can add that as well.

There's more...

The additional validators for this recipe are in the `routes.php` file for simplicity. If we were to have multiple custom validators, it might be a better idea to put them in their own validator files. To do this, we should create a file named `validator.php` in our app directory and add in any code we want. Then, open up the `global.php` file in the `app/start` directory and, at the very end of the file, add the `require app_path().'/validator.php'` function. This will load all of our validators automatically.

Building a shopping cart

E-commerce is a huge business on the web. An integral part of most e-commerce sites is the use of a shopping cart system. This recipe will walk through how to use Laravel sessions to store items for sales and build a shopping cart.

Getting ready

For this recipe, we need a standard installation of Laravel, as well as a properly set up and configured MySQL database.

How to do it...

To complete this recipe, follow these given steps:

1. In our database, create a table and add some data with this SQL code:

```sql
CREATE TABLE items (
    id int(10) unsigned NOT NULL AUTO_INCREMENT,
    name varchar(255) DEFAULT NULL,
    description text,
    price int(11) DEFAULT NULL,
    PRIMARY KEY (id)
    ) ENGINE=InnoDB;

INSERT INTO items VALUES ('1', 'Lamp', 'This is a Lamp.','14');
INSERT INTO items VALUES ('2', 'Desk', 'This is a Desk.','75');
INSERT INTO items VALUES ('3', 'Chair', 'This is a
    Chair.', '22');
INSERT INTO items VALUES ('4', 'Sofa', 'This is a
    Sofa/Couch.', '144');
INSERT INTO items VALUES ('5', 'TV', 'This is a
    Television.', '89');
```

2. In the `routes.php` file, create the routes for our cart with the following code:

```php
Route::get('items', function()
{
  $items = DB::table('items')->get();
  return View::make('items')->with('items', $items)
    >nest('cart', 'cart', array('cart_items' =>
    Session::get('cart')));
});

Route::get('item-detail/{id}', function($id)
{
  $item = DB::table('items')->find($id);
  return View::make('item-detail')->with('item', $item)
    >nest('cart', 'cart', array('cart_items' =>
    Session::get('cart')));
});

Route::get('add-item/{id}', function($id)
{
  $item = DB::table('items')->find($id);
  $cart = Session::get('cart');
  $cart[uniqid()] = array ('id' => $item->id, 'name' =>
    $item >name, 'price' => $item->price);
  Session::put('cart', $cart);
  return Redirect::to('items');
});

Route::get('remove-item/{key}', function($key)
{
  $cart = Session::get('cart');
  unset($cart[$key]);
  Session::put('cart', $cart);
  return Redirect::to('items');
});

Route::get('empty-cart', function()
{
  Session::forget('cart');
  return Redirect::to('items');
});
```

3. In the `views` directory, create a file named `items.php` with the following code:

```html
<!doctype html>
<html lang="en">
<head>
<meta charset="utf-8">
<title>Item List</title>
```

```
</head>
<body>
<div>
<?php foreach ($items as $item): ?>
<p>
<a href="item-detail/<?= $item->id ?>">
<?= $item->name ?>
</a> --
<a href="add-item/<?= $item->id ?>">Add to Cart</a>
</p>
<?php endforeach; ?>
</div>
<?php $cart_session = Session::get('cart') ?>
<?php if ($cart_session): ?>
<?= $cart ?>
<?php endif; ?>
</body>
</html>
```

4. In the `views` directory, create a file named `item-detail.php` by the given code:

```
<!doctype html>
<html lang="en">
<head>
<meta charset="utf-8">
<title>Item: <?= $item->name ?></title>
</head>
<body>
<div>
<h2><?= $item->name ?></h2>
<p>Price: <?= $item->price ?></p>
<p>Description: <?= $item->description ?></p>
<p>
<a href="../add-item/<?= $item->id ?>">Add to Cart</a>
</p>
<p><a href="../items">Item list</a></p>
</div>
<? if (Session::has('cart')): ?>
<?= $cart ?>
<? endif; ?>
</body>
</html>
```

5. In the `views` directory, create a file named `cart.php` with the following code:

```
<div class="cart" style="border: 1px solid #555">
<?php if ($cart_items): ?>
<?php $price = 0 ?>
<ul>
```

```php
<?php foreach ($cart_items as $cart_item_key =>
  $cart_item_value): ?>
<?php $price += $cart_item_value['price']?>
<li>
<?= $cart_item_value['name'] ?>:
<?= $cart_item_value['price'] ?> (<a href="remove-item/<?=
  $cart_item_key ?>">remove</a>)
</li>
<?php endforeach; ?>
</ul>
<p><strong>Total: </strong> <?= $price ?></p>
<?php endif; ?>
</div>
```

6. Now, we can go in our browser to `http://{your-server}/items` to view the list of items from our database, links to their detail pages, and an option to add them to a cart. When added to the cart, they will show at the bottom of the page.

How it works...

To begin this recipe, we need to set up a database table that will hold items that we want to add to the cart. We'll also add in a few test items, so we have some data to work with.

In our first route, we get all of the existing items in our table and display them. We're also nesting in a cart view that will show the items we already added. In that nested view, we also send in our cart session, so the list can populate.

Our next route does something similar but it accepts only one item and displays the full information.

The next route actually adds the items. First, we get the item from the database based on its ID. Then we save the existing cart session to a variable, so we can manipulate it. We add the item to the array, using php's `uniqid()` function as our key. Then we put the `cart` array back into the `Session` and redirect it.

If we want to remove an item, we first make a way to get the item's ID and remove it from the `cart` array. The other way is to just delete all the session and start over.

In our view, we'll also notice that we are only allowing the `cart` list to show if there actually is anything in the cart.

There's more...

This recipe can easily be extended to be more full-featured. For example, instead of adding a new record if we click on the same item multiple times, we could store a total number along with each item. That way, we could add a form field asking for the quantity next to the item.

Using Redis to save sessions

Redis is a popular key/value data store and is quite fast. Laravel includes Redis support, and makes it easy to interact with the Redis data.

Getting ready

For this recipe, we'll need to have a Redis server properly configured and running. More information on that can be found at `http://redis.io/`.

How to do it...

Follow these steps to complete this recipe:

1. In our `routes.php` file, create the routes as given in the following code:

```php
Route::get('redis-login', function()
{
    return View::make('redis-login');
});

Route::post('redis-login', function()
{
    $redis = Redis::connection();
    $redis->hset('user', 'name', Input::get('name'));
    $redis->hset('user', 'email', Input::get('email'));
    return Redirect::to('redis-view');
});

Route::get('redis-view', function()
{
    $redis = Redis::connection();
    $name = $redis->hget('user', 'name');
    $email = $redis->hget('user', 'email');
    echo 'Hello ' . $name . '. Your email is ' . $email;
});
```

2. In the `views` directory, create a file named `redis-login.php` with the following code:

```html
<!doctype html>
<html lang="en">
<head>
<meta charset="utf-8">
<title>Redis Login</title>
</head>
<body>
```

```
<p>
<h3>Redis Login</h3>
<?= Form::open(array('url' => 'redis-login', 'method' =>
  'post')) ?>
<?= Form::label('name', 'Your Name') ?>
<?= Form::text('name') ?>
<?= Form::label('email', 'Email') ?>
<?= Form::text('email') ?>
<?= Form::submit('Submit') ?>
<?= Form::close() ?>
</p>
</body>
</html>
```

3. Now, we can open our browser and go to http://{your-server}/redis-login and fill in the form. After submitting, we will display the information from Redis.

How it works...

Our first step is to create a simple form that we will use to input data to Redis. In our redis-login route, we use a view that will ask for a name and e-mail address and, when submitted, will post to the redis-login route.

After posting, we create a new Redis instance using the Redis::connection() function, which will use the default settings found in our app/config/database.php file. To store the information in Redis, we're using a hash and setting the data using the hset() function. Our Redis instance can use any command that Redis accepts, so we could easily choose between functions such as set() or sadd().

Once the data is in Redis, we redirect to a route that will display the data. For that, we just need to call the hget() function with the key and the field we added.

Using basic sessions and cookies

There will be times when we want to pass data from one page of our app to another page without needing to store the information in a database. To accomplish this, we can use the various Session and Cookie methods that Laravel provides us.

Getting ready

For this recipe, we need a standard Laravel installation.

How to do it...

For this recipe, follow the given steps:

1. In the `views` folder, create a file named `session-one.php` with the following code:

```
<!DOCTYPE html>
<html>
<head>
<title>Laravel Sessions and Cookies</title>
<meta charset="utf-8">
</head>
<body>
<h2>Laravel Sessions and Cookies</h2>
<?= Form::open() ?>
<?= Form::label('email', 'Email address: ') ?>
<?= Form::text('email') ?>
<br>
<?= Form::label('name', 'Name: ') ?>
<?= Form::text('name') ?>
<br>
<?= Form::label('city', 'City: ') ?>
<?= Form::text('city') ?>
<br>
<?= Form::submit('Go!') ?>
<?= Form::close() ?>
</body>
</html>
```

2. In the `routes.php` file, create our routes as given in the following code:

```
Route::get('session-one', function()
{
  return View::make('session-one');
});

Route::post('session-one', function()
{
  Session::put('email', Input::get('email'));
  Session::flash('name', Input::get('name'));
  $cookie = Cookie::make('city', Input::get('city'), 30);
  return Redirect::to('session-two')->withCookie($cookie);
});

Route::get('session-two', function()
{
  $return = 'Your email, from a Session, is '
    Session::get('email') . '. <br>';
```

```
    $return .= 'You name, from flash Session, is '
      Session::get('name') . '. <br>';
    $return .= 'You city, from a cookie, is ' .
      Cookie::get('city') . '.<br>';
    $return .= '<a href="session-three">Next page</a>';
    echo $return;
});


Route::get('session-three', function()
{
    $return = '';

    if (Session::has('email')) {
    $return .= 'Your email, from a Session, is ' .
      Session::get('email') . '. <br>';
    } else {
    $return .= 'Email session is not set.<br>';
    }

    if (Session::has('name')) {
      $return .= 'Your name, from a flash Session, is ' .
        Session::get('name') . '. <br>';
    } else {
    $return .= 'Name session is not set.<br>';
    }

    if (Cookie::has('city')) {
      $return .= 'Your city, from a cookie, is ' .
        Cookie::get('city') . '. <br>';
    } else {
      $return .= 'City cookie is not set.<br>';
    }
      Session::forget('email');
      $return .= '<a href="session-three">Reload</a>';
      echo $return;
});
```

How it works...

To begin, we create a simple form that we will use to submit information to the sessions and cookies. After posting the values, we take the `email` field and add it to a regular session. The `name` field will be added to a flash session and the `city` will be added to a cookie. Also, we'll set the cookie to expire after 30 minutes. Once they're all set, we redirect to our second page, and make sure we pass the cookie to the return value.

Our second page simply takes the values we set and displays them to verify that they were set correctly. At this point, once the request is complete, our flash session, the name, should no longer be available.

When we click on through to our third page, we add in some checks to make sure the sessions and cookies still exist, using the `has()` method on both. Our `email` and `city` should still display, but the `name` session should not. We then remove the `email` session using the `forget()` method. When we reload the page, we'll notice that the only thing that is still displayed is the `city` cookie.

There's more...

Flash data is only available on the next request we make, and then it is removed. However, if we'd like to keep our flash data, we can use the `Session::reflash()` command and it will send the data to our next request as well. If we have multiple flash data, we can also choose specific sessions to keep for the next request using the `Session::keep(array('your-session-key', 'your-other-session'))` function.

Creating a secure API server

In this recipe, we'll create a simple API to display some information from our database. To control who has access to the data, we allow users to create keys and use that key in their API request.

Getting ready

For this recipe, we need a standard installation of Laravel and a configured MySQL database.

How to do it...

To complete this recipe, we'll follow these given steps:

1. In our database, create a table to hold the API keys as given in the following code:

```
CREATE TABLE api (
  id int(10) unsigned NOT NULL AUTO_INCREMENT,
    name varchar(255) DEFAULT NULL,
    api_key varchar(255) DEFAULT NULL,
    status tinyint(1) DEFAULT NULL,
    PRIMARY KEY (id)
    ) ENGINE=InnoDB DEFAULT CHARSET=utf8;
```

2. In the database, create a table for some example data to access as shown in the following code:

```
CREATE TABLE shows (
  id int(10) unsigned NOT NULL AUTO_INCREMENT,
    name varchar(200) NOT NULL,
    year int(11) NOT NULL,
    created_at datetime NOT NULL,
    updated_at datetime NOT NULL,
    PRIMARY KEY (id)
    ) ENGINE=InnoDB CHARSET=utf8;

INSERT INTO shows VALUES ('1', 'Happy Days', '1979',
  '2013-01-01 00:00:00', '2013-01-01 00:00:00');
INSERT INTO shows VALUES ('2', 'Seinfeld', '1999',
  '2013-01-01 00:00:00', '2013-01-01 00:00:00');
INSERT INTO shows VALUES ('3', 'Arrested Development',
  '2006', '2013-01-01 00:00:00', '2013-01-01 00:00:00');
INSERT INTO shows VALUES ('4', 'Friends', '1997',
  '2013-01-01 00:00:00', '2013-01-01 00:00:00');
```

3. In the `models` directory, create a file named as `Api.php`

```php
<?php

class Api extends Eloquent {

  public $table = 'api';
  public $timestamps = FALSE;
}
```

4. In the `models` directory, create a file named as `Show.php`

```php
<?php
class Show extends Eloquent {
}
```

5. In the `views` directory, create a file named `api-key.php`

```php
<!DOCTYPE html>
<html>
<head>
<title>Create an API key</title>
<meta charset="utf-8">
</head>
<body>
<h2>Create an API key</h2>
<?php echo Form::open() ?>
<?php echo Form::label('name', 'Your Name: ') ?>
<?php echo Form::text('name') ?>
<br>
<?php echo Form::submit('Go!') ?>
<?php echo Form::close() ?>
```

```
</body>
</html>
```

6. In the `routes.php` file, create the routes to allow for the `api-key` registration

```php
Route::get('api-key', function() {
  return View::make('api-key');
});

Route::post('api-key', function() {
  $api = new Api();
  $api->name = Input::get('name');
  $api->api_key = Str::random(16);
  $api->status = 1;
  $api->save();
  echo 'Your key is: ' . $api->api_key;
});
```

7. In the `routes.php`, create the routes for accessing the `api` by the following code:

```php
Route::get('api/{api_key}/shows', function($api_key)
{
  $client = Api::where('api_key', '=', $api_key)->where('status',
'=', 1)->first();
  if ($client) {
  return Show::all();
  } else {
  return Response::json('Not Authorized', 401);
  }
});
Route::get('api/{api_key}/show/{show_id}', function($api_key,
$show_id)
{
  $client = Api::where('api_key', '=', $api_key)->where('status',
'=', 1)->first();
  if ($client) {
  if ($show = Show::find($show_id)) {
  return $show;
  } else {
  return Response::json('No Results', 204);
  }
  } else {
  return Response::json('Not Authorized', 401);
  }
});
```

8. To test it out, in the browser, go to `http://{your-server}/api-key` (where `{your-server}` is the name of the development server) and fill in the form. On the next page, copy the key that was generated. Then, go to `http://{your-server}/api/{your-copied-key}/shows` and a list of shows should appear in the `json` format.

How it works...

We begin by setting up our tables and models. Our API table will be used to check for the key and the `show` table will be the test data we will use the key to access.

Our next task is to create a way to generate keys for our application. In this example, we'll only take a name value. After submitting, we create a random, 16-character string that will be the user's key. We then save the information to the table and display the key to the user.

To use this key, we create two routes to display the information. The first route uses the `{api_key}` wildcard in the URL, and passes that value to our function. We then query the database for that key and make sure the status is still active. This way, if we decide to revoke a user's key, we can set the status to false and they won't be able to use the API. If they don't exist or the status is false, we respond with the HTTP code of 401, to show that they aren't authorized. Otherwise, we return the Eloquent object that will allow us to display the records in the `json` format.

Our second route will display the records of a single show. For that URL, we use the `{api_key}` wildcard for the key and the `{show_id}` wildcard for the ID of the show. We pass those to the functions, and then check the key as before. If the key is valid, we make sure a show with that ID exists, and use the Eloquent object again to display only the show with the given ID in the `json` format.

There's more...

We also have the option of using a Laravel filter, if we'd rather have the api keys posted instead. To do that, we'd create a new filter in the `filters.php` file

```
Route::filter('api', function()
{
  if ($api_key = Input::get('api_key')) {
  $client = Api::where('api_key', '=', $api_key)-
    >where('status', '=', 1)->first();
  if (!$client) {
  return Response::json('Not Authorized', 401);
}
  } else {
  return Response::json('Not Authorized', 401);
}
});
```

And then, for our `shows` routes, we respond to a post request and add the `before` filter as shown in the following code:

```
Route::post('api/shows', array('before' => 'api', function()
{
  return Show::all();
}));
```

10
Testing and Debugging Your App

In this chapter, we will cover:

- ▸ Setting up and configuring PHPUnit
- ▸ Writing and running a test case
- ▸ Using Mockery to test controllers
- ▸ Writing acceptance tests using Codeception
- ▸ Debugging and profiling your app

Introduction

As web applications grow more complex, we need to make sure that any changes or updates we make to the existing code won't negatively affect other parts of code. One way to check for this is to create unit tests. Laravel provides very helpful ways for us to include unit tests with our app.

Setting up and configuring PHPUnit

In this recipe, we'll see how to install and setup the popular PHPUnit testing package: PHPUnit.

Getting ready

For this recipe, we need a working installation of Laravel 4. We'll also need the Composer dependency tool installed from `http://getcomposer.org`.

How to do it...

To complete this recipe, follow the given steps:

1. In the root directory of the application, add the following line to the composer.json file:

   ```
   "require-dev": {
   "phpunit/phpunit": "3.7.*"
   },
   ```

2. Open the command line window, navigate to the root directory, and run an update on the Composer tool with the following line:

   ```
   php composer update
   ```

3. After it is installed, run a quick test in the command line window with the command:

   ```
   vendor/bin/phpunit
   ```

How it works...

Our composer.json file tells the Composer tool which packages it should install. So our first task is to add the phpunit package as a requirement. After saving that file, we'll run an update command and phpunit will be added to our vendor directory.

After it's installed, we can run the command to test out phpunit and make sure it was installed correctly. Laravel comes with an example test case in the app/tests directory, and it should pass all tests.

Writing and running a test case

In this recipe, if we already have the PHPUnit installed and working, we can write a test case and use PHPUnit to check if it is valid or not.

Getting ready

To run a test case, we'll need a working installation of Laravel. We'll also need to have installed PHPUnit from the previous recipe, *Setting up and configuring PHPUnit*.

How to do it...

To complete this recipe, follow the given steps:

1. In the `app/tests` directory, create a file named `MyAppTest.php` with the following code:

```php
<?php
class MyAppTest extends TestCase {

    /**
     * Testing the MyApp route
     *
     * @return void
     */
    public function testMyAppRoute()
    {
        $response = $this->call('GET', 'myapp');
        $this->assertResponseOk();
        $this->assertEquals('This is my app', $response
        >getContent());
    }
}
```

2. Run the tests in the command line window, and we should get failing tests on entering the following command:

    vendor/bin/phpunit

3. In our `routes.php` file, add a new route with the following code:

```php
Route::get('myapp', function()
{
    return 'This is my app';
});
```

4. Run the test again to get a passing unit test

    vendor/bin/phpunit

How it works...

When we run our PHPUnit tests, Laravel will automatically look in the `app/tests` directory. We begin by creating a new file in that directory to hold the test named as `MyAppTest` and extend `TestCase`.

For this simple test, we use the `call` method and do a `GET` request on the `myapp` route. The first thing we check for is that we receive an `Ok` or a `200` status code, and then that the content returned is the string `This is my app`. At this point, when we run the test, it will fail because we haven't created the route yet.

Next, we create our `myapp` route and return the string `This is my app`. Finally, we re-run the test and we should get a successful result.

See also

▶ The *Setting up and configuring PHPUnit* recipe

Using Mockery to test controllers

Sometimes, we need to test the code that uses our database. The commonly accepted practice is that we shouldn't actually do live queries on the database while running a unit test. To get around this, we can use the Mockery package to fake our data.

Getting ready

For this recipe, we need to have Laravel installed and working, as well as PHPUnit from the *Setting up and configuring PHPUnit* recipe.

How to do it...

To complete this recipe, follow the given steps:

1. Open up our `composer.json` file, and make sure the following code is included:

```
"require-dev":
{
  "phpunit/phpunit": "3.7.*",
  "mockery/mockery": "dev-master"
},
```

2. Open the command line terminal and run the Composer update with the following command:

```
php composer.phar update
```

3. After the update, in the `app/controllers` directory, create the `ShipsController.php` file using the following code:

```php
<?php

class ShipsController extends BaseController {
```

```php
    protected $ships;
    public function __construct(Spaceship $ships)
    {
      $this->ships = $ships;
    }

    public function showShipName()
    {
      $ship = $this->ships->first();
      return $ship->name;
    }
    }
```

4. In `routes.php` file, add a route to this controller using the following command line:

   Route::get('ship', 'ShipsController@showShipName');

5. In the `app/tests` directory, create a file named as `SpaceshipTest.php` as shown in the following code:

```php
<?php

class SpaceshipTest extends TestCase {

    public function testFirstShip ()
    {
      $this->call('GET', 'ship');
      $this->assertResponseOk();
    }
    }
```

6. Back in the command line window, run our tests with the following command:

   vendor/bin/phpunit

7. At this point, we will get a failing test that displays the following message:

   ReflectionException: Class Spaceship does not exist

8. Since the `Spaceship` class is going to be our model, we'll use Mockery to mock it. Update the `SpaceshipTest` class with the following code:

```php
<?php

class SpaceshipTest extends TestCase {

    public function testFirstShip()
    {
      $ship = new stdClass();
      $ship->name = 'Enterprise';
```

```
$mock = Mockery::mock('Spaceship');
$mock->shouldReceive('first')->once()->andReturn($ship);

$this->app->instance('Spaceship', $mock);
$this->call('GET', 'ship');
$this->assertResponseOk();
}


    public function tearDown()
{
    Mockery::close();
}
}
```

9. Now, back in the command line window, run the test again and it should pass.

How it works...

We begin by installing the Mockery package using the Composer. This will allow us to use it throughout our application. Next, we create a controller with one method that will display the name of a single ship. In the controller's constructor, we pass in the model we want to use, and in this case it's going to be named Spaceship and use Laravel's Eloquent ORM.

In the showShipName method, we'll get the first record from the ORM, then do a simple return of the record's name. We then need to make a route that points to the controller and the showShipName method.

When we first create the test, we simply make a GET request and see if it sends back an OK response. At this point, since we haven't made out the Spaceship model yet, it will display an error when we run the test. We could add the needed tables to the database and create the model, and the test would pass. However, when testing controllers, we don't want to worry about the database and should only be testing whether the controller code is working. For that, we can now use Mockery.

When we call the first method on the Spaceship class, it will give us an object holding all the returned fields, so we first create a generic object and assign it to the $ship controller. Then, we create our mock object for the Spaceship class and, when our controller asks for the first method, the mock object will return our previously created generic object.

Next, we need to tell Laravel that whenever the Spaceship instance is requested, it should use our mock object instead. And finally, call GET on our ship route and make sure it returns an OK response.

See also

▶ The *Setting up and configuring PHPUnit* recipe

Writing acceptance tests using Codeception

Acceptance testing is a useful way to test that your application is outputting the correct information to the browser. Using a package such as Codeception, we can automate these tests.

Getting ready

For this recipe, we'll need a working copy of Laravel installed.

How to do it...

To complete this recipe, follow the given steps:

1. Open the `composer.json` file, and add the following line to our `require-dev` section:

    ```
    "codeception/codeception": "dev-master",
    ```

2. Open the command line window, and update the app with the following command:

    ```
    php composer.phar update
    ```

3. After it is installed, we need to run the `bootstrap` command in the terminal, as shown in the following command:

    ```
    vendor/bin/codecept bootstrap app
    ```

4. In the `app/tests/acceptance` directory, create a file named as `AviatorCept.php` using the following code:

    ```php
    <?php

    $I = new WebGuy($scenario);
    $I->wantTo('Make sure all the blueprints are shown');
    $I->amOnPage('/');
    $I->see('All The Blueprints');
    ```

5. In our main `routes.php` file, update the default route using the following code:

    ```php
    Route::get('/', function()
    {
    return 'Way of the future';
    });
    ```

6. Open the command line window and run the acceptance test with the following command:

    ```
    vendor/bin/codecept run -c app
    ```

7. At this point, we should see it failing. To make it pass, update the default route once more by entering the following code:

```
Route::get('/', function()
{
return 'All The Blueprints';
});
```

8. In the command line window, run the test again using the following command:

   vendor/bin/codecept run -c app

9. This time, it should pass.

How it works...

We start by installing the Codeception package through the Composer. Once it's downloaded, we run the `bootstrap` command that will create all the needed files and directories. Codeception automatically adds the files and folders to a `tests` directory; thus, to make sure they are added into Laravel's test directory, we add the `app` directory to the end of the `bootstrap` command.

Next, we create the file to hold our test in the `acceptance` directory. We start by creating a new `WebGuy` object, which is Codeceptions class to run acceptance tests. The next line is describing what we want to do, which in this case is to see all the blueprints. The next line tells the test which page we need to be on, which will correspond to our routes. For our purposes, we're just checking the default route. Finally, we tell the test what we want to `see` on the page. Any text we put here should be displayed somewhere on the page.

Our first pass at the default route will display `Way of the future`; thus, when the Codeception test is run, it will fail. To run the tests, we use the `run` command and make sure we use the `-c` flag and specify the `app` as the path to the tests, since we installed the bootstrap files inside the `app/tests` directory.

Then, we can update the route to display the text `All The Blueprints` and re-run the test. This time, it will pass.

There's more...

Codeception is a very powerful testing suite with many different options. To fully understand everything it can do, go to `http://codeception.com/`.

Debugging and profiling your app

If we want to know how our application is working behind the scenes, we'll need to profile it. This recipe will show how to add in a profiler to our Laravel app.

Getting ready

For this recipe, we'll need a working copy of Laravel with a MySQL database properly configured.

How to do it...

To complete this recipe, follow the given steps:

1. Open up the command line window and use the `artisan` command to create our migrations as given in the following code:

   ```
   php artisan migrate::make create_spaceships_table -create -
   table="spaceships"
   ```

2. In the `app/database/migrations` folder, open the file whose name begins with the date and ends with `create_spaceships_table.php`, and use this for our database table

   ```php
   <?php

   use Illuminate\Database\Schema\Blueprint;
   use Illuminate\Database\Migrations\Migration;

   class CreateSpaceshipsTable extends Migration {

       /**
        * Run the migrations.
        *
        * @return void
        */
       public function up()
       {
           Schema::create('spaceships', function(Blueprint $table)
       {
           $table->increments('id');
           $table->string('name');
           $table->string('movie');
           $table->timestamps();
       });
       }
   ```

```php
/**
 * Reverse the migrations.
 *
 * @return void
 */
public function down()
{
  Schema::drop('spaceships');
}


}
```

3. In the `app/database/seeds` folder, create a file named `SpaceshipSeeder.php` as shown in the following code:

```php
<?php

class SpaceshipSeeder extends Seeder {

  /**
   * Run the database seeds.
   *
   * @return void
   */
  public function run()
{
  DB::table('spaceships')->delete();

  $ships = array(
  array(
  'name'    => 'Enterprise',
  'movie'   => 'Star Trek'
),
  array(
  'name'    => 'Millenium Falcon',
  'movie'   => 'Star Wars'
),
  array(
  'name'    => 'Serenity',
  'movie'   => 'Firefly'
),
  );

  DB::table('spaceships')->insert($ships);
}
}
```

4. In the same directory, open the `DatabaseSeeder.php` file and make sure the `run()` method looks like the following snippet:

```php
public function run()
{
  Eloquent::unguard();
  $this->call('SpaceshipSeeder');
}
```

5. Back in the command line window, install the migration and run the seeder with the following code:

```
php artisan migrate

php artisan db:seed
```

6. In the `app/models` directory, create a file named as `Spaceship.php` as shown in the following snippet:

```php
<?php

class Spaceship extends Eloquent{

  protected $table = 'spaceships';
}
```

7. In the `app/controllers` directory, create a file named as `ShipsController.php`

```php
<?php

class ShipsController extends BaseController {

  protected $ships;

  public function __construct(Spaceship $ships)
  {
  $this->ships = $ships;
}

  public function showShipName()
{
  $ships = $this->ships->all();
  Log::info('Ships loaded: ' . print_r($ships, TRUE));
  return View::make('ships')->with('ships', $ships);
}
}
```

8. In the `routes.php` file, register the route as shown in the following command:

   ```
   Route::get('ship', 'ShipsController@showShipName');
   ```

9. In the `app/views` directory, create a view named as `ships.blade.php` as shown in the following code:

   ```
   @foreach ($ships as $s)
   {{ $s->name }} <hr>
   @endforeach
   ```

10. At this point, if we go to the `http://{your-dev-url}/public/ship`, we'll see the list of ships. Next we need to open the `composer.json` file and add the following line in the `require-dev` section:

    ```
    "loic-sharma/profiler": "dev-master"
    ```

11. Then in the command line window, update the Composer using the following command:

    ```
    php composer.phar update
    ```

12. After everything is downloaded, in the `app/config` folder, open the `app.php` file. In the `providers` array, add the following line to the end of the code:

    ```
    'Profiler\ProfilerServiceProvider',
    ```

13. In the same file, in the `aliases` array, add the following line:

    ```
    'Profiler' => 'Profiler\Facades\Profiler',
    ```

14. At the top of this file, make sure `debug` is set to true, then go back to `http://{your-dev-url}/public/ship` in your browser. The `profiler` will show up at the bottom of the browser window.

How it works...

Our first step is to create the page we want to profile. We start with using the `artisan` command to create a `migrations` file, and then add in the Schema builder code to make our spaceships table. When that's done, we can add some information to the table using the seeder file.

With that complete, we can now run the migration and the seeder, and our table will be created with all the information already populated.

Next we create a simple model and a controller for our data. In the controller, we'll simply get all of the ships and pass the variable to our ships view. We'll also add a logging event in the middle of the code. This will allow us to debug the code later, if we need to.

Once that's done, we can see the list of ships we created.

Then, we need to install the profiler package, which is based on a previous version of Laravel's profiler. After updating our Composer file, we then register the profiler so our app knows of its existence; we also register the Façade if we want to do more with it later.

In our config file, if we have debug set to TRUE, the profiler will display on every page we access. We can disable the profiler by simply setting debug to FALSE.

There's more...

We could also add timers to our app using the startTimer and endTimer methods as shown in the following snippet:

```
Profiler::startTimer('myTime');
{some code}
Profiler::endTimer('myTime');
```

11
Deploying and Integrating Third-party Services into Your Application

In this chapter, we will cover:

- ▶ Creating a queue and using Artisan to run it
- ▶ Deploying a Laravel app to Pagoda Box
- ▶ Using the Stripe payment gateway with Laravel
- ▶ Doing a GeoIP lookup and setting custom routing
- ▶ Gathering e-mail addresses and using them with a third-party e-mail service
- ▶ Storing and retrieving cloud content from Amazon S3

Introduction

Web applications will often rely on third-party services to help our applications run. Using Composer and Laravel, we can integrate existing code that will allow us to interact with these services. In this chapter, we'll see how to deploy our app to Pagoda Box, use Stripe payments, do GeoIP lookups, use a third-party e-mail service, and store the content to the cloud.

Creating a queue and using Artisan to run it

There may be times when our app is required to do a lot of work behind the scenes to accomplish a task. Instead of making a user wait until the tasks are complete, we can add them to a queue and do the processing later. There are many queue systems available but Laravel has a few that are very easy to implement. In this recipe, we'll be using IronMQ.

Getting ready

For this recipe, we'll need a working installation of Laravel 4, as well as API credentials for IronMQ. A free account can be created at `http://www.iron.io/`.

How to do it...

To complete this recipe, follow the given steps:

1. In the `app/config` directory, open the `queue.php` file, set the default value to `iron` and fill in the credentials from IronMQ.

2. Open Laravel's `composer.json` file and update the required section so it looks resembles the following snippet:

   ```
   "require": {
   "laravel/framework": "4.0.*",
   "iron-io/iron_mq": "dev-master"
   }
   ```

3. In the command line window, update the composer file with the following command:

   ```
   php composer.phar update
   ```

4. After everything is installed, open the `routes.php` file and create a route that hits the queue:

   ```
   Route::get('queueships', function() {
   $ships = array(
     array(
       'name' => 'Galactica',
       'show' => 'Battlestar Galactica'),
       array(
       'name' => 'Millennium Falcon',
       'show' => 'Star Wars'),
       array(
       'name' => 'USS Prometheus',
       'show' => 'Stargate SG-1')
   );
   ```

```php
$queue = Queue::push('Spaceship', array('ships' =>
$ships));
  return 'Ships are queued.';
});
```

5. Create a file in the `app/models` directory with the name `Spaceship.php` as shown in the following code:

```php
<?php

class Spaceship extends Eloquent{

  protected $table = 'spaceships';

  public function fire($job, $data)
  {
// Could be added to database here!
    Log::info('We can put this in the database: ' .
      print_r($data, TRUE));
    $job->delete();
  }
}
```

6. In your browser, go to `http://{your-url}}/public/queueships`, and refresh a couple of times.

7. Check in the IronMQ window that new messages were added.

8. Open up the command line window and run the following command:

   php artisan queue:listen

9. After a few moments, look inside the folder `app/storage/logs` and find the file with today's date in the name. It will have a print out of the array we added to the queue.

How it works...

We begin by making sure to use IronMQ as our default queue driver, in the `config` file. If we wanted to use another queue system, we could set that here. Then we install the IronMQ package into our application, using composer. This will add all the files we need, as well as any dependencies that Iron needs to work.

At this point, Laravel is already set up to use whatever queue system we choose, so we can begin using it. We first create an array of data in our route. This could just as easily be form input, so some other data we'd like to wait to process. We then use the `Queue::push()` method, set the class that should be used (`Spaceship`), and then pass in the data to send to that class.

If we now go to this route and then check the IronMQ queue, we'll see that there's one job waiting to be processed. Our next task is to create a class to process the queue. For that, we create a model named `Spaceship`. We need to create a `fire()` method to parse our data from the queue. Here, we could save the information to a database or do some other heavy processing. For now, we'll just send the data to a log file. At the end of the `fire()` method, we make sure to delete the job.

If we go to our `queueships` route and refresh a few times, we'll see multiple jobs in our queue, but we haven't processed them yet. Therefore, in the command line, we run artisan's `queue:listen` command, and this will start processing our queues. Pretty soon, we can go into our logs directory, and see the information that was sent from the queue.

There's more...

There are many reasons we might want a queue. Most often it's for things such as processing images or doing heavy data parsing. It's also useful to queue any e-mails we want to send from the site, and Laravel has a special way to do that using the `Mail::queue()` command.

Deploying a Laravel app to Pagoda Box

Pagoda Box is a popular cloud hosting service that makes creating a web app very easy. With pre-made boxes for Laravel, we can create our own site in the cloud.

Getting ready

For this recipe, we need to have a free account with Pagoda Box, which is available at `https://dashboard.pagodabox.com/account/register`. After signing up, we'll also need to have an SSH key added to our account. More information about the SSH keys can be found at `http://help.pagodabox.com/customer/portal/articles/202068`.

How to do it...

To complete this recipe, follow the steps given:

1. After logging in to Pagodabox, click on the **New Application** tab as shown in the following screenshot:

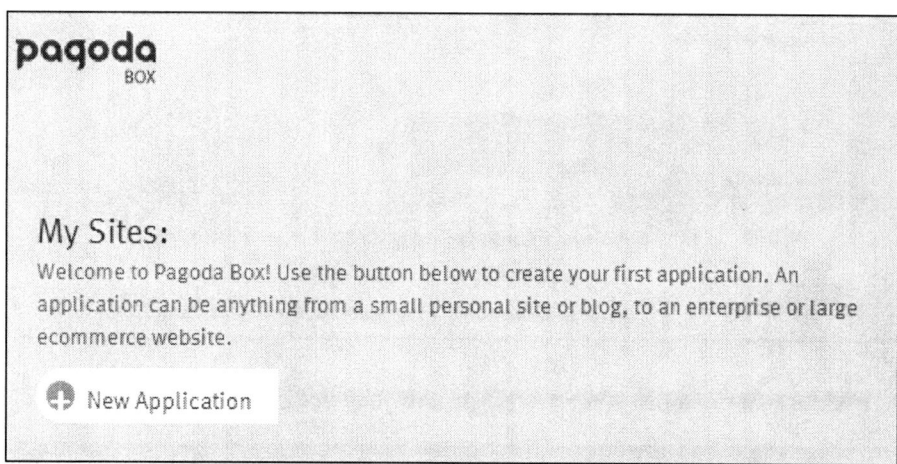

2. Make sure **Quickstart** is selected, then scroll down to find the laravel-4 quickstart. The click on the **Free** button as shown in the following screenshot:

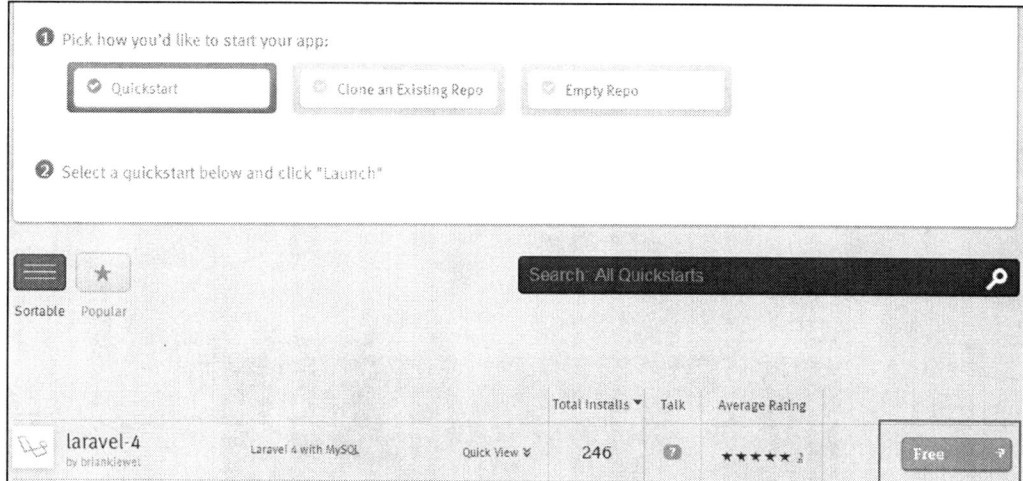

3. On the next page, click on the **Launch** button as shown in the following screenshot:

4. Wait for a few minutes while everything gets installed.

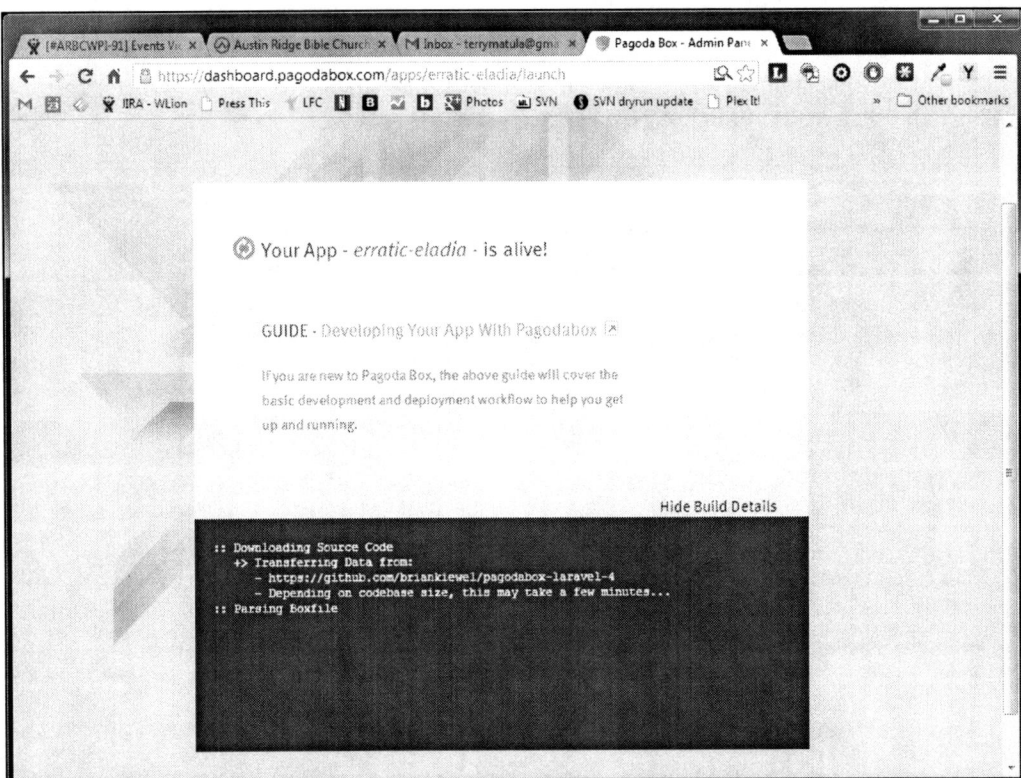

5. Once it's finished, click on the blue **Manage Your App** button as shown in the following screenshot:

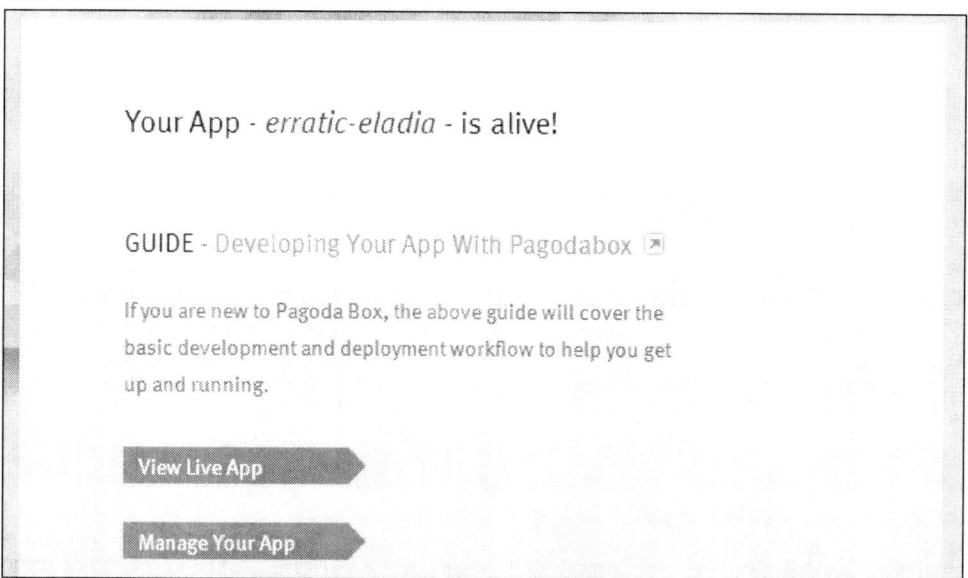

6. Copy the git clone URL as shown in the following screenshot:

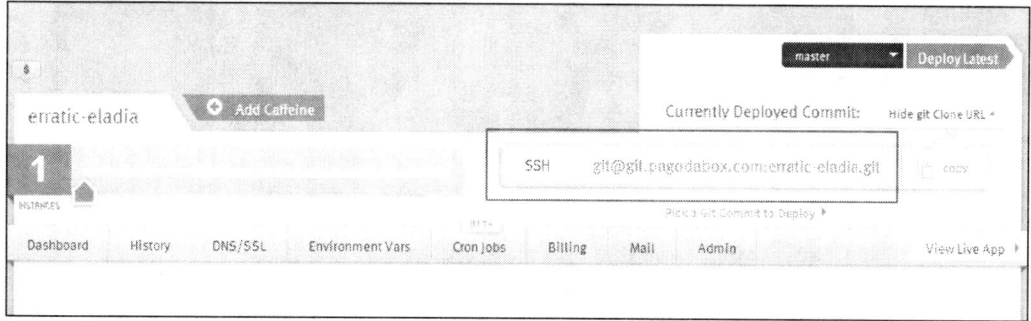

7. In the command line window, go to the root of your server and run the git clone command. In our case, it would be:

```
git clone git@git.pagodabox.com:erratic-eladia.git pagodaapp
```

8. After everything downloads, open the app/routes.php file and add a route so we can test it out as given in the following code:

```
Route::get('cool', function()
{
  return 'Pagoda Box is awesome!';
});
```

9. In the command line window, commit the following changes and send it back to the Pagoda Box

```
git commit -am 'Added route'
git push origin master
```

10. After Pagoda Box has finished the changes, go to the new route to see if it works. In our case, it will be `http://erratic-eladia.gopagoda.com/cool`.

How it works...

If we want to host our app and make sure it's scalable, we might want to look at a cloud hosting service. This will let us increase its performance if we happen to get an influx of traffic, and lower it when the traffic dies down. An excellent host that works well with PHP and Laravel is Pagoda Box. Pagoda Box also has a very nice free option that will allow us to test it out and create a full app without needing to pay.

To begin with, in the Pagoda Box dashboard, we create a new application and choose a Quickstart package we want to use. In the list is a handy Laravel 4 installation; if we choose it, everything will be installed for us, including all the dependencies.

After everything is set up, we can copy the git clone code and download the files to our local server. Once it's downloaded, we can do any updates and commit them. After pushing it back to Pagoda Box, our updated code will automatically be deployed and we will see the changes on the live site.

There's more...

There are other cloud hosting providers that work well with Laravel. They tend to all have free options so we can try them out. Some other hosts are as follows:

- ▸ Engine Yard `https://www.engineyard.com/`
- ▸ Digital Ocean `https://www.digitalocean.com/`
- ▸ Heroku (there's hidden PHP support) `https://www.heroku.com/`

Using the Stripe payment gateway with Laravel

E-commerce sites are a consistent staple in web development. In the past, things such as credit card processing have been difficult and the learning curve very steep. With Laravel and the Stripe service, offering credit card transactions is much easier.

Getting ready

For this recipe, we'll need a working installation of Laravel 4 and the proper credentials for Stripe. A free account with Stripe can be created at `https://stripe.com/`.

How to do it...

To complete this recipe, follow these steps:

1. Open the app's `composer.json` file and update the `require` section to resemble the following snippet:

    ```
    "require": {
      "laravel/framework": "4.0.*",
      "stripe/stripe-php": "dev-master"
    },
    ```

2. In the command line window, run the composer update with the following command:

    ```
    php composer.phar update
    ```

3. In the `app/config` directory, create a new file named `stripe.php` with the following code:

    ```php
    <?php

    return array(
        'key' => 'fakeKey-qWerTyuuIo4f5'
    );
    ```

4. In the `routes.php` file, add a `Route` to the payment form as shown in the following code:

    ```php
    Route::get('pay', function()
    {
        return View::make('pay');
    });
    ```

5. In the `app/views` folder, create a file named `pay.blade.php` for our form using the following snippet:

    ```
    {{ Form::open(array('url' => 'pay', 'method' => 'post')) }}
    Card Number: {{ Form::text('cc_number',
        '4242424242424242') }}<br>

    Expiration (month):
      {{ Form::select('cc_exp_month', array(1 => '01', 2 =>
      '02', 3 => '03', 4 => '04', 5 => '05',6 => '06', 7 =>
      '07', 8 => '08', 9 => '09', 10 => '10', 11
      => '11', 12 => '12')) }}<br>
    ```

```
Expiration (year):
  {{ Form::select('cc_exp_year', array(2013 => 2013,
  2014 => 2014, 2015 => 2015, 2016 => 2016)) }}<br>


{{ Form::submit('Charge $37 to my card') }}
{{ Form::close() }}
```

6. Back in the `routes.php`, create a `Route` to accept the form post, and charge the card as given in the following code:

```
Route::post('pay', function()
{
  Stripe::setApiKey(Config::get('stripe.key'));
  $chargeCard = array(
    'number' => Input::get('cc_number'),
    'exp_month' => Input::get('cc_exp_month'),
    'exp_year'  => Input::get('cc_exp_year')
);
  $charge = Stripe_Charge::create(array('card' =>
    $chargeCard, 'amount' => 3700, 'currency' => 'usd'));

// Save returned info here
  var_dump($charge);
});
```

How it works...

We start with adding the Stripe package to our composer files and updating it. This will install the Stripe code, as well as any dependencies if it requires. Then we need to create a configuration file to hold our API key. Here we could create another directory that's the same as our environment variable, and add that file there. So, if we have a development and a production server, we could have a Stripe `config` file in the `app/config/development` directory that holds our test API key, and then in the `app/config/production` directory a file to hold our live API key.

Next, we need a form for the user to enter their credit card information. We create a pay route that displays our pay view. In that view, we'll use the Blade template for creating the form. The minimum that Stripe requires is the card number and the expiration date, though there might be times we need to capture the card's CVV code or the user's address.

After that form is posted, we create an instance of Stripe with the API key. Then we add the credit card information to an array. Finally, we send the amount (in cents), the card array, and the currency to Stripe for processing.

The data returned from Stripe could then be added to a database, or otherwise tracked.

There's more...

Stripe offers many, easy-to-use methods for managing credit card transactions, or even things such as subscriptions. For more information, be sure to check out the documentation available on: `https://stripe.com/docs`

Doing a GeoIP lookup and setting custom routing

There might be times when our app needs to give people different pages depending on which country they're in. Using Laravel and MaxMind's GeoIP data, we can lookup a person's country, based on their IP address, and then redirect them to the page we need.

Getting ready

For this recipe, we'll just need a working Laravel 4 installation.

How to do it...

To complete this recipe, follow these steps:

1. Open the `composer.json` file and update the `require` section, so it looks like the following snippet:

```
"require": {
  "laravel/framework": "4.0.*",
  "geoip/geoip": "dev-master"
},
```

2. In the command line window, run the composer update with the following command:

```
php composer.phar update
```

3. Go to `http://dev.maxmind.com/geoip/legacy/geolite/` and download the latest **GeoLite Country** database. Unzip it and put the `GeoIP.dat` file in the root of our app.

4. In the `app/config` directory, create a file named `geoip.php` with the following code:

```php
<?php

return array(
  'path' => realpath("path/to/GeoIP.dat")
);
```

5. Open the `app/filters.php` file and add a filter for our `geoip` file with the following code:

```
Route::filter('geoip', function($route, $request, $value
    = NULL)
{
  $ip = is_null($value) ? Request::getClientIp() : $value;
  $gi = geoip_open(Config::get('geoip.path'),
    GEOIP_STANDARD);
  $code = geoip_country_code_by_addr($gi, $ip);
  return Redirect::to('geo/' . strtolower($code));
});
```

6. In our `routes.php` file, create a route to apply the filter to and a route to accept the country code, as shown in the following code:

```
Route::get('geo', array('before' => 'geoip:80.24.24.24',
function()
{
return '';
}));
Route::get('geo/{country_code}', function($country_code)
{
return 'Welcome! Your country code is: ' . $country_code;
});
```

How it works...

We begin this recipe by installing the `geoip` library, by adding it to our `composer.json` file and updating. Once it's downloaded, we can then download MaxMind's free `geoip` data file and add it to our app. In our case, we'll put the file in the root of our app. Then, we need to create a `config` file that will hold the location of the `geoip` data file.

Next, we want to check the user's IP address and redirect them to a country specific page. For this, we'll use Laravel's before filter. It starts by setting the `$ip` variable. If we manually pass in an IP address, that's what it will use; otherwise, we run the `Request::getClientIp()` method to try and determine it. Once we have the IP address, we run it through the `geoip` function to get the country code for the IP address. We then redirect the user to the route with the country code as a parameter.

Then we create a route to add the filter to. In our case, we'll pass an IP address manually to the filter, but if it wasn't there it would attempt to use the user's address. Our next route takes the country code as a parameter. At this point, we could offer custom content based on the country or even automatically set which language file to use.

Gathering e-mail addresses and using them with a third-party e-mail service

E-mail lists and newsletters are still a popular and efficient way to communicate with large groups of people. In this recipe, we'll use Laravel and the free MailChimp service to set up an easy way to gather e-mail subscriptions.

Getting ready

For this recipe, we'll need a working Laravel 4 installation, as well as a free account with `http://mailchimp.com/` and generated API keys in Mailchimp's account section. We'll also need to create at least one list in Mailchimp.

How to do it...

To complete this recipe, follow these steps:

1. In the `app` directory, create a new directory named `libraries`.

2. Download Mailchimp's API library from `http://apidocs.mailchimp.com/api/downloads/#php`, then unzip it and place the file `MCAPI.class.php` in the new `libraries` folder.

3. Open Laravel's `composer.json` file and add the libraries directory to the `autoload` section. That section should resemble the following snippet:

```
"autoload": {
  "classmap": [
  "app/commands",
  "app/controllers",
  "app/models",
  "app/database/migrations",
  "app/database/seeds",
  "app/tests/TestCase.php",
  "app/libraries"
]
},
```

4. Open the command line window, and run the composer's `dump-autoload` command, as shown in the following command:

```
php composer.phar dump-autoload
```

5. In the `app/config` directory, create a file named `mailchimp.php` with the following code:

```php
<?php

return array(
  'key' => 'mykey12345abcde-us1',
  'list' => 'q1w2e3r4t5'
);
```

6. To get all of our Mailchimp lists, and see their IDs, open the `routes.php` file and add a new route as shown in the following code:

```php
Route::get('lists', function()
{
  $mc = new MCAPI(Config::get('mailchimp.key'));
  $lists = $mc->lists();

  if($mc->errorCode) {
    echo 'Error loading list: ' . $mc->errorMessage;
  } else {
    echo '<h1>Lists and IDs</h1><h3>Total lists: '
    $lists['total'] . '</h3>';
  foreach($lists['data'] as $list) {
    echo '<strong>' . $list['name'] . ':</strong> ' .
    $list['id'] . '<br>';
  }
  }
});
```

7. In `routes.php` file, create a route to show the `subscribe` form using the following code:

```php
Route::get('subscribe', function()
{
  return View::make('subscribe');
});
```

8. In `app/views` directory, create a file named `subscribe.blade.php` as given in the following snippet:

```php
{{ Form::open() }}
First Name: {{ Form::text('fname') }} <br>
Last Name: {{ Form::text('lname') }} <br>
Email: {{ Form::text('email') }} <br>
{{ Form::submit() }}
{{ Form::close() }}
```

9. In the `routes.php` file, create a route to accept and process the form submission as given in the following code:

```
Route::post('subscribe', function()
{
  $mc = new MCAPI(Config::get('mailchimp.key'));

  $merge_vars = array('FNAME' => Input::get('fname'),
    'LNAME' => Input::get('lname'));
  $ret = $mc->listSubscribe(Config::get('mailchimp.list'),
    Input::get('email'), $merge_vars);

if ($mc->errorCode){
  return 'There was an error: ' . $mc->errorMessage;
} else {
  return 'Thank you for your subscription!';
}
});
```

How it works...

To begin this recipe, we'll need to add Mailchimp's PHP library. Since we won't be using a composer, we need to set up a directory to hold any of our non-composer libraries. So we create a `libraries` directory in the `app` folder, and add Mailchimp there.

To let Laravel know that we want to `autoload` anything in the new directory, we need to update the `composer.json` file. We then add the directory location to the `Classmap` section. Then we need to run composer's `dump-autoload` command to recreate our `autload` files, and have it added in our new directory.

We then need to create a new `config` file to hold our Mailchimp credentials and the ID of the list we want to use. We can get the `list` ID from the Mailchimp dashboard, or we can use the `lists` route to display them all.

To capture the user's e-mail, we create a route and view to hold our form. This form could also be in a pop-up, modal, or part of a larger page. We ask for their name and e-mail, and then have it posted to Mailchimp.

In our `post` route, we just need to instantiate the Mailchimp class, create an array to hold the name, and send everything to the `listSubscribe()` method. Finally, we check for any errors from Mailchimp and show a success message.

There's more...

Mailchimp offers a very extensive API that allows us to easily manage our e-mail lists. To see everything they offer, check out the online documentation at: `http://apidocs.mailchimp.com/`

Storing and retrieving cloud content from Amazon S3

Using a service such as Amazon's S3 to store our files will allow us to leverage their servers' speed and reliability. To utilize the service, we can easily implement a Laravel package to handle our uploads to Amazon.

Getting ready

For this recipe, we'll need a working Laravel 4 installation. We'll also need a free Amazon AWS account, which can be registered at: `http://aws.amazon.com/s3/`

After registering, we need to get our **Access Key ID** and **Secret ID** from the **Security Credentials** page. Also, in the S3 management console, we'll need to have at least one bucket created. For this recipe, we'll call the bucket named as `laravelcookbook`.

How to do it...

To complete this recipe, follow the given steps:

1. Open Laravel's `composer.json` file and add the Amazon SDK package. The require section should resemble the following snippet:

   ```
   "require": {
     "laravel/framework": "4.0.*",
     "aws/aws-sdk-php-laravel": "dev-master"
   },
   ```

2. Open the command line window, and install the package using the Composer package, as given in the following code:

   ```
   php composer.phar update
   ```

3. After everything is installed, in the `app/config` directory, create a file named as `aws.php` shown in the following code:

   ```
   <?php

   return array(
     'key'    => 'MYKEY12345',
   ```

```
'secret' => 'aLongS3cretK3y1234abcdef',
'region' => '',
);
```

4. In the app/config directory, open the app.php file. At the end of the providers array, add the AWS provider as given in the following code:

```
'Aws\Laravel\AwsServiceProvider',
```

5. Also in the app.php file, in the aliases array, add the following alias:

```
'AWS' => 'Aws\Laravel\AwsFacade',
```

6. In our routes.php files, test that everything is working by creating a route to list our buckets with the following code:

```
Route::get('buckets', function()
{
  $list = AWS::get('s3')->listBuckets();
    foreach ($list['Buckets'] as $bucket) {
    echo $bucket['Name'] . '<br>';
}
});
```

7. To test the buckets, go to http://{your-server}/buckets, and it should display a list of all of the buckets we've set up.

8. Now let's create a form for a user to upload an image. We begin with a route to hold the form as given in the following code:

```
Route::get('cloud', function()
{
  return View::make('cloud');
});
```

9. In the app/views folder, create a file named as cloud.blade.php with the following code:

```
{{ Form::open(array('files' => true)) }}
Image: {{ Form::file('my_image') }} <br>
{{ Form::submit() }}
{{ Form::close() }}
```

10. Back in the routes.php file, create a route to process the file and upload it to S3 as shown in the following code:

```
Route::post('cloud', function()
{
  $my_image = Input::file('my_image');
  $s3_name = date('Ymdhis') . '-' . $my_image
    >getClientOriginalName();
  $path = $my_image->getRealPath();
```

```
$s3 = AWS::get('s3');
$obj = array(
   'Bucket'     => 'laravelcookbook',
   'Key'        => $s3_name,
   'SourceFile' => $path,
   'ACL'        => 'public-read',
);

if ($s3->putObject($obj)) {
return
   Redirect::to('https://s3.amazonaws.com/laravelcookbook/
   ' . $s3_name);
} else {
return 'There was an S3 error';
}
});
```

How it works...

We begin the recipe by installing Amazon's AWS SDK. Thankfully, Amazon released a composer package specifically designed for Laravel 4, so we just add that to our `composer. json` file and update.

After everything is installed, we need to create a configuration file and add in our Amazon credentials. We can also add in the `region` (such as `Aws\Common\Enum\ Region::US_WEST_2`) but, if we leave it blank, it will use the `US Standard` region. Then we update our `app.php` configuration, including the AWS `ServiceProvider` and the `Facade` that Amazon provided.

If we already have buckets in our S3, we can create a route to list those buckets. It begins by creating a new S3 instance and simply calling the `listBuckets()` method. We then loop through the array of `Buckets` and show their name.

Our next goal is to create a form where a user can add an image. We create the `cloud` route that displays the `cloud` view. Our view is a simple Blade template form with a single `file` field. That form will then be posted to `cloud`.

In our `cloud` post route, we begin by retrieving the image using the `Input::file()` method. Next, we create a new name for our image by adding the date to the beginning of the file's name. Then we get the path of the uploaded image, so we know which file to send to S3.

Next, we create an S3 instance. We also need an array to hold the values to send to S3. `Bucket` is simply the name of the S3 bucket we want to use, `Key` is the name we want to give to the file, `SourceFile` is the location of the file we want to send over, and then `ACL` are the permissions we want to give to the file. In our case, we set `ACL` to `public-read`, which allows the image to be displayed to anyone.

Our final step is to call the `putObject()` method which should send everything to our S3 bucket. If it's successful, we then redirect the user to view the uploaded file.

There's more...

In our example, the user is forced to wait until the image is uploaded to Amazon before continuing. This would be an excellent case to use a queue to process everything.

See also

> ▸ The *Creating a queue and using Artisan to run it* recipe

Index

Thank you for buying
Laravel Application Development Cookbook

About Packt Publishing

Packt, pronounced 'packed', published its first book "*Mastering phpMyAdmin for Effective MySQL Management*" in April 2004 and subsequently continued to specialize in publishing highly focused books on specific technologies and solutions.

Our books and publications share the experiences of your fellow IT professionals in adapting and customizing today's systems, applications, and frameworks. Our solution based books give you the knowledge and power to customize the software and technologies you're using to get the job done. Packt books are more specific and less general than the IT books you have seen in the past. Our unique business model allows us to bring you more focused information, giving you more of what you need to know, and less of what you don't.

Packt is a modern, yet unique publishing company, which focuses on producing quality, cutting-edge books for communities of developers, administrators, and newbies alike. For more information, please visit our website: www.packtpub.com.

About Packt Open Source

In 2010, Packt launched two new brands, Packt Open Source and Packt Enterprise, in order to continue its focus on specialization. This book is part of the Packt Open Source brand, home to books published on software built around Open Source licences, and offering information to anybody from advanced developers to budding web designers. The Open Source brand also runs Packt's Open Source Royalty Scheme, by which Packt gives a royalty to each Open Source project about whose software a book is sold.

Writing for Packt

We welcome all inquiries from people who are interested in authoring. Book proposals should be sent to author@packtpub.com. If your book idea is still at an early stage and you would like to discuss it first before writing a formal book proposal, contact us; one of our commissioning editors will get in touch with you.

We're not just looking for published authors; if you have strong technical skills but no writing experience, our experienced editors can help you develop a writing career, or simply get some additional reward for your expertise.

[PACKT] PUBLISHING open source
community experience distilled

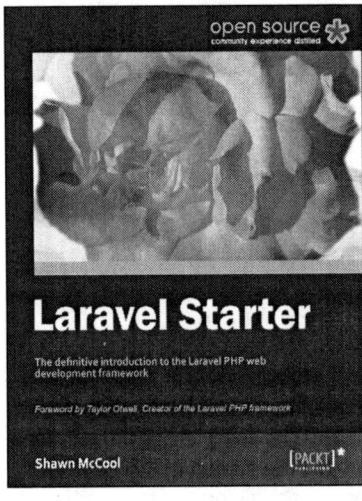

Laravel Starter [Instant]

ISBN: 978-1-78216-090-8   Paperback: 64 pages

The definitive introduction to the Laravel PHP web development framework

1. Learn something new in an Instant! A short, fast, focused guide delivering immediate results

2. Create databases using Laravel's migrations

3. Learn how to implement powerful relationships with Laravel's own "Eloquent" ActiveRecord implementation

4. Learn about maximizing code reuse with the bundles

Laravel Application Development Blueprints

ISBN: 978-1-78328-211-1   Paperback: 299 pages

Learn to develop ten fantastic applications with the new and improved Laravel 4

1. Learn how to integrate third-party scripts and libraries into your application

2. With different techniques, learn how to adapt different methods to your needs

3. Expand your knowledge of Laravel 4 so you can tailor the sample solutions to your requirements

Please check **www.PacktPub.com** for information on our titles

CodeIgniter for Rapid PHP Application Development

ISBN: 978-1-84719-174-8   Paperback: 260 pages

Improve your PHP coding productivity with the free compact open-source MVC CodeIgniter framework!

1. Clear, structured tutorial on working with CodeIgniter

2. Careful explanation of the basic concepts of CodeIgniter and its MVC architecture

3. Using CodeIgniter with databases, HTML forms, files, images, sessions, and email

4. Building a dynamic website quickly and easily using CodeIgniter's prepared code

Instant Zend Framework 2.0

ISBN: 978-1-78216-412-8   Paperback: 52 pages

Leverage the power of Zend Framework to build practical MVC applications

1. Learn something new in an Instant! A short, fast, focused guide delivering immediate results

2. Discover how to get the skeleton application

3. Configure the skeleton application to use Zend Framework 2

4. Understand how to validate forms, and upload files using Zend Framework 2

Please check **www.PacktPub.com** for information on our titles

CPSIA information can be obtained at www.ICGtesting.com
Printed in the USA
LVOW09s1345220614

391141LV00009B/302/P